ACTIVITIES FOR
ECONOMICS
EDUCATION

F. Barton Truscott

J. WESTON

WALCH
PUBLISHER
Portland, Maine

User's Guide
to
Walch Reproducible Books

As part of our general effort to provide educational materials that are as practical and economical as possible, we have designated this publication a "reproducible book." The designation means that purchase of the book includes purchase of the right to limited reproduction of all pages on which this symbol appears:

Here is the basic Walch policy: We grant to individual purchasers of this book the right to make sufficient copies of reproducible pages for use by all students of a single teacher. This permission is limited to a single teacher and does not apply to entire schools or school systems, so institutions purchasing the book should pass the permission on to a single teacher. Copying of the book or its parts for resale is prohibited.

Any questions regarding this policy or requests to purchase further reproduction rights should be addressed to:

Permissions Editor
J. Weston Walch, Publisher
321 Valley Street • P.O. Box 658
Portland, Maine 04104-0658

1   2   3   4   5   6   7   8   9   10

ISBN 0-8251-3924-4

CONTENTS

How to Use This Book v

Activities

1. The Power of Economics: Costs, Benefits, and Logic 1

2. Scarcity in the Real World, and the Resulting Tradeoffs 5

3. Ins and Outs 8

4. The Specialists 11

5. You and the Business Do Business . . . Twice! 14

6. Money Makes the Economy Go 'Round! 18

7. Markets and Prices Rule! 21

8. Demand and Supply: The Meaning 24

9. Demand and Supply: The Meeting 28

10. Demand and Supply: Dynamic, Not Static 32

11. Different Kinds of Markets: From Competition to Monopoly 38

12. Savings and Banks, a Key Economic Institution 43

13. More Key Players and Key Economic Institutions 47

14. Government: *The* Key Economic Institution 53

15. Gross Domestic Product (GDP): Everything Plus
    the New Kitchen Sink 59

16. Inflation: The Dollar's Biggest Enemy Has a Few Friends 64

17. Unemployment: Who's Working and Who Isn't 69

18. Fiscal and Monetary Policy: Directing the Economy to
    an Ideal Level 72

19. International Currency Exchange: Dollars and Sense 76

Appendices

Appendix I: A Very Different Kind of Stock Market Project 82

Appendix II: Finally, Understanding Interest and Interest Rates 84

Appendix III: Calculating Inflation:
Your Own Personal Consumer Price Index (CPI) 86

Appendix IV: Calculating Unemployment:
Your Own Local Unemployment Rate 88

HOW TO USE THIS BOOK

Economics is more—a lot more—than most students think, more than they can learn from classroom textbooks, more than they can get from the news. And it's a lot more than most economists can tell them! While textbooks, newspapers, and economists can and do teach your high school students important things about the study of economics, they often neglect to show the really good stuff, the stuff that excites, the stuff that works. For example, most texts don't stress enough the following truths about economics:

- Economics is all around us.

- We use economics in our own lives even when we don't realize it.

- Economics is great fun!

This supplemental text is designed to go beyond what most classroom texts give you and your students. Those texts give you the cake; we'll put on the icing.This text will enable you to bring economics to life for your students—individually and in groups, in class and out. Projects are based on real-life situations and may include Internet applications that can be completed by anyone using a computer with Internet access. Students will experience for themselves the power, the excitement, and the reach of economics both in their lives and in virtually every corner of our society. This text is a hands-on manual, best used in conjunction with your principal classroom text. Teach the theory using your main text; then open this book to the fascinating things students can do—and learn—with economics, including these:

- how to decide whether to go to college or start working;

- why professional athletes and movie stars make astounding salaries;

- how to fill out a tax return . . . and what the government does with your money;

- how concert tickets, shoes, and imported cars are priced.

To complete most activities in this book, students will need writing materials and access to a computer, either in or out of class, with access to the World Wide Web. Any additional materials for an activity will be specified.

Each activity consists of a teacher guide page and several reproducible student activity pages. Each teacher guide page includes: a lesson summary, educational objectives for the activity, the economics background for the activity, directions for presenting the activity, time needed, assessment and evaluation, and further applications for the material. If materials other than paper and pencil are required for the activity, a list of materials is also included on the teacher page.

Each student section consists of several distinct parts. The first is The Bottom Line, a summary of the economics principle being addressed. In Personal Economics, students see examples of how key economic concepts affect individuals. The Beyond the Bottom Line section offers projects that require students to put the principles into action. The final part of each student section is Internet Economics, which prompts students to find specific economics concepts at work on the Internet.

Before presenting any activity to your students, be sure to read through the student pages. To ensure that students understand the projects, detailed directions for many of the activities are included on the student pages. You should familiarize yourself with these projects before assigning them.

Whether a student decides to continue studying economics in college or calls it quits after this course, economics can be an enormously valuable tool. So help your students take their first step in the study of economics, a discipline that may change forever the way they look at the world.

About the Author

F. Barton Truscott has taught introductory economics and advanced placement (AP) courses for over a decade at Harvard School and Cate School in California. He currently teaches at Charles Wright Academy in Tacoma, Washington. At all three schools, he originated, developed, and was the first to teach the AP economics curriculum. Over 90 percent of his students have earned 3s or better on the advanced placement examinations in micro- and macroeconomics, thereby qualifying for advanced placement or college credit at most colleges and universities. Mr. Truscott earned his B.A. from Wesleyan University and his M.A.T. from Occidental College. Prior to entering teaching, he was an investment banker.

ACTIVITY 1
THE POWER OF ECONOMICS: COSTS, BENEFITS, AND LOGIC

Lesson Summary

The essence of economics is logic.

Objectives

- Students will recognize that we all think, reason, and decide economically—that is to say, logically—even if we don't realize it.

Background

When we have a decision to make or an objective to fulfill, we (1) consider the available options, (2) calculate the expected costs (–) and benefits (+) of each option, and (3) choose the option that we hope will yield the greatest value. This model of logical decision making is the essence of economics, since it can help us explain and predict nearly all manner of human behavior. Throughout our study of economics, we will assume that people, acting as consumers, business people, and even as representatives of the government, act logically.

Directions

1. Have students read The Bottom Line. Briefly explore meaning and significance in their own lives.

2. Have students read and complete the Personal Economics example in class.

3. Compare tables. Is there one best way to pick up Grandmother at the airport? (No—each individual has his/her own options, expected costs and benefits, net values, and corresponding "best" course of action.)

4. Assign students the Internet Economics application for homework. This assignment asks students to find interesting, **reputable** web sites and explain logically why someone would go to the trouble of developing and maintaining those sites, even when anyone can access them for free.

Time Needed

1–2 class periods

Assessment and Evaluation

Collect Internet Economics assignments from all students. To what extent did they complete the assignment (using correct addresses) and show that they understood the rule and power of logical decision making as it applies to web masters?

Further Applications

The scope of logical decision making is virtually limitless. Ask students to come up with more examples of decisions, large or small, that they make logically, even if they don't realize it. In fact, can students think of any decisions they make where they do not internally calculate the costs and benefits of available options to make the logical choice? Are there any exceptions to the rule of logical decision making? Was Hitler logical? Is love logical? Are drug addicts logical? (To the last three questions, I would argue "yes," but it's fun to debate.) How does money fit into the concept of logical decision making? (Costs and benefits are often, though not always or even necessarily, measured in dollars.)

 **Web Sites**

www.yale.edu

1

Name_____ Date_____

◆ THE POWER OF ECONOMICS: COSTS, BENEFITS, AND LOGIC ◆

The Bottom Line

People base decisions on what they expect their costs and benefits to be. We all calculate this in our own minds, with **costs** counting **negatively** and **benefits** counting **positively**. First we weigh the costs and benefits. Then we choose the option that gives us the **greatest net value** (benefits minus costs). People do what they think makes the most sense in a given situation. They act logically. (Of course, this does not mean that everyone acts the same, or that logically made decisions are always right—just that they're logical!)

Personal Economics

Here's an example of the costs and benefits of an action. I need to pick up my grandmother at the airport. The airport is 10 miles away, and my grandmother is 102 years old. I have several options: walk, drive, send her cab fare, charter a limo, or leave her stranded. To make a decision, I think of the costs and benefits of each option. Then I weigh them against each other (benefits minus costs) to come up with a net value.

In this case, the first option—walking—is a poor option for me, not to mention for my grandmother. I'll assign this option a low net value. The second option, driving, rates a much higher net value on my internal scoreboard: It's fast and

relatively easy. In the table below, I have outlined the costs, benefits, and net value of these two options.

Which option should I choose? If you said, "The option that makes the most sense," you're right. We all do that, even if we don't realize it. We subtract the costs from the benefits and calculate a net value for each option. Then we choose the option that gives the greatest net value.

In this case, even though I didn't fill in the costs and benefits of the other three options (send her cab fare, charter a limo, or leave her stranded), I decide that the second option, driving, yields the highest net value of all the possible options. This is the same as saying, "It's the option that makes the most sense."

How would you fill out the Pick up Grandmother table? On the next page there is another version of the table, with all the options, but no costs, benefits, or net values. Fill it in according to your own scoreboard. What would be the costs and benefits of each option *as they apply to you*? Which option would you choose to pick up *your* grandmother at the airport?

OBJECTIVE: PICK UP GRANDMOTHER AT THE AIRPORT			
Options	**Costs (–)**	**Benefits (+)**	**Net Value**
Walk	Takes time, energy Lots of luggage to carry Grandmother is 102	Great exercise	Low
Drive	Gas and parking costs Accident risk Potential for heavy traffic	Comfortable ride Relatively fast	High

(continued)

       Activities for Economics Education

Name_____ Date_____

◆ THE POWER OF ECONOMICS: COSTS, BENEFITS, AND LOGIC ◆ *(continued)*

OBJECTIVE: PICK UP GRANDMOTHER AT THE AIRPORT			
Options	**Costs (–)**	**Benefits (+)**	**Net Value**
Walk			
Drive			
Send cab fare			
Charter a limo			
Leave her stranded			
Other: _____ _____			

🌐 *Beyond the Bottom Line*

Think of two decisions you need to make today. On a separate piece of paper, make up a form like the one below. List the decision you need to make at the top. List all the possible choices you could make under Options. Then list the costs and benefits of each choice, and calculate the net value of each one. Which is the best option for you? Finally, write one or two sentences to justify your choice.

DECISION:			
Options	**Costs (–)**	**Benefits (+)**	**Net Value**
Option/Decision chosen: Justification:			

(continued)

© 2000 J. Weston Walch, Publisher

Activities for Economics Education

◆ THE POWER OF ECONOMICS: COSTS, BENEFITS, AND LOGIC ◆ *(continued)*

Internet Economics

It's tough to find a place on the Web where logical decision making is not taking place. Many sites on the Internet are free. They are designed to spread news about a person or a group. One example is **www.yale.edu**. This site is designed to post news about a school, Yale University. For every site on the Web, someone has decided that the benefits of creating the site (increased sales, greater publicity) are greater than the costs (paying a web master to design and build the site, maintaining the site).

Find at least three interesting, reputable sites on the Web. Why do you think the web masters of these sites spent the time and money to develop them? Name three web sites, with proper addresses. Offer specific reasons why each site may have been developed.

Site #1: _____

Reasons for development: _____

_____

_____

_____

_____

Site #2: _____

Reasons for development: _____

_____

_____

_____

_____

Site #3: _____

Reasons for development: _____

_____

_____

_____

_____

ACTIVITY 2
SCARCITY IN THE REAL WORLD, AND THE RESULTING TRADEOFFS

Lesson Summary

Scarcity is a fact of life for everyone, everywhere. We all have to make tough decisions— and tradeoffs—about what we consume, what we make, and what we do.

Objectives

- Students will demonstrate an understanding of the role scarcity plays as individuals, businesses, and government representatives make difficult tradeoffs, giving up one thing to get or do another. They will also see the different priorities of Democrats and Republicans in terms of government programs, and the tradeoffs political parties are willing to make.

Directions

1. Have students read The Bottom Line and complete Personal Economics. Discuss meaning and significance of scarcity and tradeoffs; compare individual lists of "wants."

2. Assign Beyond the Bottom Line and Internet Economics for homework. For Beyond the Bottom Line, most students should be familiar with the kinds of programs that the government pays for, but if they're stuck, they should start Internet Economics right away. All of the web sites listed, but particularly the Republican and Democratic party web sites at www.rnc.org and www.democrats.org, offer a wealth of information about government programs and whether they should be funded.

Time Needed

2 class periods

Assessment and Evaluation

Collect Beyond the Bottom Line and Internet Economics assignments from each student. In Beyond the Bottom Line, how specific were students in listing government programs, and how persuasive were their rationales for funding—or eliminating—certain programs? In Internet Economics, how accurately did students identify programs that Republicans/Democrats tend to support?

Further Applications

The following questions are good springboards for additional discussion. Is Bill Gates, a man who has $50 billion, really plagued by scarcity? (Yes—especially when you consider that "time" is probably a very scarce resource for him.) Are all goods "scarce"? (I think so; one possible exception is "air," a commodity available in unlimited quantities everywhere at absolutely no cost, although *clean* "air" does raise questions of cost.) As a follow-up to Beyond the Bottom Line and Internet Economics, you may want students to try their own hand at balancing the federal budget and seeing firsthand the difficult tradeoffs required—which programs to keep and which programs to axe—using the University of California's budget simulation game at www.garnet.berkeley.edu.

 Web Sites

www.rnc.org
www.democrats.org
www.concordcoalition.org

Name_____ Date_____

◆ SCARCITY IN THE REAL WORLD, AND THE RESULTING TRADEOFFS ◆

 ### *The Bottom Line*

In the imperfect world we live in, none of us, even the wealthy, have enough of the things we want. We seem to have **unlimited wants** (prosperity, clean air) and **scarce resources** (productive land, employable workers). Some people and countries, do, of course, have more than others. However, all of us feel we don't have enough of what we want. We are reluctant to make

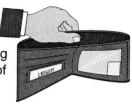

tradeoffs. But getting one thing often means not getting something else. The value of the option you gave up is called **opportunity cost**. Scarcity and tradeoffs are indeed an unfortunate fact of life.

 ### *Personal Economics*

Make a list of your wants—things you'd like more of, or just some of. Many people would say "money," but be specific. What things would you buy with more money? Use the line below and the back of this sheet, if needed.

_____

Are there also things you'd like that can't be bought with money? What about time, or more knowledge? Anything else? List them below and on the back of this sheet, if needed.

_____

 ### *Beyond the Bottom Line*

Did you know that the U.S. government spends well over $1 trillion every year on goods and services and still doesn't have enough to satisfy everyone? Yes, even our government has to deal with scarcity and make tradeoffs. That's why Congress and the president have such a battle every year over the budget and who gets what. Consider this question: What are some of the competing demands for government money?

If you're stuck, look at the newspaper or news programs or the Internet. Invariably, you can find stories about people arguing about how government money—*your* money paid in taxes—should be spent. What is *your* opinion on some of these programs? Add more programs to the list below. Then say whether or not you think each one should be funded.

Government Program	My Opinion
1. Money to make health care more affordable for all elderly	
2. Money to increase our military security and international presence	
3.	
4.	
5.	

(continued)

Activities for Economics Education

Name_____ Date_____

◆ SCARCITY IN THE REAL WORLD, AND THE RESULTING TRADEOFFS ◆ *(continued)*

Circle the programs you feel most deserve government money. Now, unless you want higher taxes or a budget deficit (where the government spends more money than it has) you'll need to make some tradeoffs. Which government programs should be cut to pay for the ones you support? For every program you support, name an existing one that must be axed. Be specific. Make sure you explain *why* you want to make this tradeoff.

Internet Economics

The federal budget is a great place to see unlimited wants fighting for scarce resources. As the budget takes shape, the two political parties battle daily over how our tax money should be spent. The Republican party has its own web page detailing and promoting its budget positions (**www.rnc.org**). So do the Democrats (**www.democrats.org**). There's also a nonpartisan group called The Concord Coalition (**www.concordcoalition.org**). This group claims to analyze federal budget issues with more neutrality and a longer-term perspective. Check out these web sites. Then answer the following questions:

1. List five specific federal programs and the official Democratic and Republican positions on each.

Program	Democratic Position	Republican Position
1.		
2.		
3.		
4.		
5.		

2. What kind of programs do the Democrats tend to support? What kind of programs do the Republicans tend to support?

_____

_____

_____

3. What tradeoffs would the Democrats be willing to make in order to pay for the kinds of programs they support? What tradeoffs would the Republicans be willing to make to pay for the kinds of programs they support?

_____

_____

_____

ACTIVITY 3
INS AND OUTS

Lesson Summary

Producers assemble land, labor, and capital (**inputs**) to produce goods or services (**outputs**) that are sold to consumers. This activity builds on the concepts of scarce resources and unlimited wants introduced in Activity 2.

Objectives

- Students will demonstrate an understanding of the outlines of our market structure where producers use inputs to make outputs and sell them to consumers.

Directions

1. Have students read and complete The Bottom Line and Personal Economics. Make sure students understand the definition of *capital* (often misused) and the difference between a good and a service.

2. Commence the in-class group project described in Beyond the Bottom Line, following the directions carefully. There will be some running around initially, as students are first assigned designations of land, labor, or capital and then herded into one of four groups. Once the groups are set, the members of each group should choose a good or service and then assign roles/ specific assignments so that this good or service can realistically be produced. Allow about 15 minutes for groups to complete this task, which includes putting their specific plans to paper. Then give each group time (two–three minutes each) to make a short presentation to the whole class. Whichever group does the best job— in your judgment or according to a class vote—of setting up a realistic production plan using each of the inputs and explaining how each input works earns a prize, extra credit, etc. (whatever you decide).

3. Assign Internet Economics as a homework project. Tell students to be prepared to share results of their homework during the next class.

Time Needed

1–2 class periods

Assessment and Evaluation

Since the Beyond the Bottom Line is designed for groups and is conducted in class, it affords you a good opportunity to assess how well students interact and cooperate with each other. In particular, groups and individuals can be graded on the quality of their oral presentation, their specific contributions to the project, and their general enthusiasm. You can collect and check the Internet economics assignment, or simply ask students to share their results.

Further Applications

How can capital be both an input *and* an output? (A machine that makes bottles is a capital good—an input—helping to make glass bottles in the future. It's also a piece of equipment that was first produced and sold to a consumer, in this case, the bottling plant. Thus, it was an output *before* it became an input.)

 Web Sites

www.coldwellbankercommercial.com
www.studentsource.com
www.ipodata.com//

◆ INS AND OUTS ◆

 ## The Bottom Line

In the second activity, we talked about scarce resources and unlimited wants. Let's put some names and definitions to those concepts.

I. **Inputs**: Scarce productive resources, or **inputs**—so called because they go *into* producing something—can typically be divided into three types: **land**, **labor**, and **capital**.

Land is the very ground we walk on. Land can be used to grow crops. Land can also be used to build a factory or an office building or a sports arena. In economics, land can also be used to describe a natural resource, such as oil or water.

Labor is the work, physical or mental, that is needed to make something. You may need a field to grow crops, but you also need someone to plant the seeds, irrigate the field, and harvest the crops.

Capital is money or machinery or some other productive resource (other than land or labor) used to produce goods and services *in the future*.

II. **Outputs**: Outputs are the results of productively combining land, labor, and capital. There are two types:

Goods are objects that can satisfy people's wants: a Ford Mustang, a CD player, an orange.

Services are actions that can satisfy people's wants: a massage, an hour of legal services, a night at the movies.

III. **Consumers and Producers**: Consumers are the people who buy the goods and services. They buy them from producers, the people who make them from the inputs listed above.

 ## Personal Economics

So land, labor, and capital (inputs) are essential for producing any good or service (outputs), like a bushel of wheat, or a Camaro, or a year of college tuition. For example, one acre of land plus one farmer plus one tractor plus seed (inputs) produce one bushel of corn (output). Try to think of some good or service you like or use.

What inputs—land, labor, capital—go into making it? Then start the following group project.

Beyond the Bottom Line

The teacher will divide the class into temporary groups of land, labor, and capital. Within each group, count off by 4s. Remember your input and your number ("I'm land, number 2" or "I'm capital, number 4").

Now move into four *new* groups determined by number: all of the 1s, all of the 2s, etc., in different corners of the classroom. Each group (1s, 2s, 3s, and 4s) should include people representing each of the inputs. Some should represent land. Some should represent labor. The rest should represent capital. Each group's mission is to choose a good or service, then assign specific roles so that good or service can be produced.

(continued)

Name_____ Date_____

◆ INS AND OUTS ◆ *(continued)*

For example, let's say Group 3 chooses to produce pencils. Its *land* members are responsible for buying or renting the land where trees are cut down to provide wood for the pencils. They also need to obtain the land on which to build a factory, etc. Its *labor* members are responsible for hiring workers to cut down the trees, run the factories, sell the pencils, etc. Its *capital* members are responsible for obtaining the equipment needed to cut down trees, make the pencils in the factories, ship the product to the stores, etc. Finally, each group should list the specific roles and responsibilities of each of its inputs on paper, as shown below, and present its plan to the whole class.

OUTPUT	INPUTS		
Good/Service	Land	Labor	Capital
Pencils	Land where trees are cut down Land for factory	Lumberjacks Factory workers Salesmen	Chain saws Trucks Pencil-making machines

 Internet Economics

There are literally millions of outputs (goods and services) on the Web. If you want to see inputs (land, labor, capital), too, in action on the Web, check out the following:

- **www.coldwellbankercommercial.com** to see commercial real estate for sale for development (land)

- **www.studentsource.com** for job placements of students and recent graduates (labor)

- **www.ipodata.com** for news of companies raising money through public stock offerings for the purposes of expanding or developing their business (capital)

See if you can find more examples of land, labor, and capital on the Web. List specific addresses and give short explanations.

Inputs:

- Land—Web address: _____

  Explanation: _____

  _____

- Labor—Web address: _____

  Explanation: _____

  _____

- Capital—Web address: _____

  Explanation: _____

  _____

ACTIVITY 4
THE SPECIALISTS

Lesson Summary

People specialize and pool their different talents so that they can produce much more together than they ever could individually.

Objectives

- Students will see firsthand that specialization raises production and our quality of life well above subsistence level.

Background

Specialization also breathes life into the economic structure introduced in Activity 3, where producers make goods and services from scarce inputs and sell them to consumers.

Directions

1. Have students read The Bottom Line and read and complete Personal Economics. Discuss. How many individuals are, or could learn to be, completely self-sufficient?

2. Commence the in-class Beyond the Bottom Line project, following the directions carefully. It will be a bit rowdy, so alert teachers next door if noise poses a problem. Afterwards, discuss the pros and cons of specialization (assembly-line production is extremely efficient, but can be dull for workers).

3. Assign Internet Economics as a homework project.

Time Needed

1–2 class periods

Assessment and Evaluation

Collect the Internet Economics homework assignment. See how well students understand the concept of specialization by assessing how successfully and persuasively each matches his or her specific talents, real or imagined, with the responsibilities of the job desired. Assess their written plea with a grade and/or a simple, "You're (not) hired!"

Further Applications

It's not just specialization that drives the economic "engine": Advancing technology and developing human capital—improving workers' skills—are two additional forces behind sustained increases in economic productivity. These powerful forces have enabled companies to produce and sell more goods and services, earn higher profits, and pay their workers higher salaries even as they work fewer hours. Ask students to cite examples of advancing technology and ways that workers can and do improve their skills.

 Web Sites

www.microsoft.com

◆ THE SPECIALISTS ◆

💰 *The Bottom Line*

People perform different tasks—they **specialize**—and pool their talents so that they can produce more together than they could individually.

🖩 *Personal Economics*

Consider this question: How many things—goods and services—do you personally consume in a day? Go ahead—make a list:

Goods and services I will consume today:

_____

_____

_____

_____

_____

_____

_____

Compare your list to a friend's. Did you leave anything out? Chances are that you came up with a pretty long list, once you thought about all the different kinds of food you eat, clothes you wear, appliances you use—and that's just for starters!

Now, how many of those goods and services could you produce *on your own*? List them here.

_____

_____

_____

_____

_____

_____

Be honest. It's a much shorter list, isn't it? My list is tiny. I can't hunt or sew, and I'm a terrible cook. So, how do we do it—live, and live pretty well, even though most of us don't have the skills to survive on our own? The answer is **specialization of labor**. We make and sell the things we're good at making and buy what we need (and want) with the money we earn.

(continued)

◆ THE SPECIALISTS ◆ (continued)

📊 *Beyond the Bottom Line*

Warning: This will be very noisy and very silly! At the classroom auto plant, cars can be made in four steps. Each step is completed in a different corner of the room in this order:

1. At the first corner, jump up and down four times.

2. Now, move to a different corner and do three sit-ups (or three windmills).

3. Now, move to a different corner and do two push-ups.

4. Finally, move to the last corner and sing the alphabet once.

In the first part of this activity, you will work as a solo producer. You have exactly five minutes to see how many "cars" you can make on your own. Write down the results.

Number of cars made as solo producer: _____

Next, the teacher will arrange everyone into four-person groups. Each group will assign its members a different job. When the teacher says "go," those assigned to job 1 start jumping up and down; those assigned to job 2 start doing sit-ups, and so forth. Try to go as fast as you can without making mistakes! Now, record how many cars your group built in exactly five minutes.

Number of cars made as part of a team: _____

Compare group results to individual results. Who produced more? What did you learn about group production and specialization? What are the pros and cons of assembly-line production?

💻 *Internet Economics*

Examples of specialization abound on the Internet and wherever job openings are posted. At the Microsoft (**www.microsoft.com**) web site, job openings are listed, and they tend to be very specialized. For example, Microsoft was recently looking for a "financial analyst." This person's qualifications should include a minimum of six years experience in finance or accounting "in a large distributed computer operations environment." It's clear that Microsoft was not looking for someone to do it all, but for a specific person to undertake a defined, specialized responsibility. Entry-level jobs—jobs typically open to people with little or no experience—are usually not quite as specialized. However, companies often train or groom these new workers to fill specialized positions fairly quickly.

See if you can find a job advertised on the Web that you would like to have. Identify the job, the employer, the specific responsibilities, the necessary qualifications, and the salary, if listed. Explain exactly why you would like to have this job and why you think you'd be good at it. What specialized skills do you have that would make you the right person for the job? Pretend your prospective employer will read what you wrote. If it's convincing enough, you're hired! Finally, in a separate paragraph, write down what you would do with the money you earned from this job.

Web address: _____

Position advertised: _____

Employer: _____

Qualifications: _____

_____

Salary: _____

I want this job because: _____

_____

I would be good at this job because: _____

_____

My skills: _____

_____

Lesson Summary

The two key players in our economy, the individual and the business, interact on two very important levels: the buying and selling of outputs (goods and services) through the use of prices; and the buying and selling of inputs (land, labor, capital) through the use of rent, wages, and interest. Both the individual and the business are motivated to do business with each other because they *both* stand to gain from voluntary transactions.

Objectives

- Students will see that the Double Circular Flow Model sets into motion the structure, the players, and the concepts studied up to this point and that it describes the economy as it is—in perpetual motion. Students will also see that the economy is about more than just the buying and selling of goods and services; it is also about the buying and selling of land, labor, and capital, where the individual and the business swap their traditional roles as buyer and seller.

Directions

1. Have students read The Bottom Line and read and complete Personal Economics. If students have questions about interest, refer to Activity 12 or Appendix II. Make certain students understand two key concepts: (1) the Double Circular Flow Diagram and (2) the mutually beneficial exchange between buyer and seller.

2. Assign Beyond the Bottom Line and Internet Economics for homework.

3. Have students share the results of their Beyond the Bottom Line homework in the following class. After completing this project, they should understand that professional sports team owners and Hollywood producers have a very good, and logical, reason for paying huge salaries to their stars: They—the owners and producers—expect to benefit from having such a person under contract.

Time Needed

1–2 class periods

Assessment and Evaluation

Collect Beyond the Bottom Line and Internet Economics homework. For the first assignment, assess how well students understand the concept of a mutually beneficial transaction in their justification of the payment of a huge salary to a star. For the Internet Economics homework, see if students can find and summarize the selling of various inputs—land, labor, and capital—on the Net.

Further Applications

An additional discussion question might be, "Are *all* transactions between buyers and sellers mutually advantageous?" Most are, in a free market. However, sometimes buyers and/or sellers have few, if any, adequate options, or outcomes do not occur as planned.

 Web Sites

www.alliedcapital.com
www.hia.com/rockctr/

◆ You and the Business Do Business . . . Twice! ◆

The Bottom Line

Now that we understand the basic concepts, we are ready to learn how our American economy works. In other words, how and why do the **individual**, also known as **household/consumer**, and the **business**, also known as the **firm/producer**, interact?

How: As you can see in the Double Circular Flow Diagram below, the individual and the business work together on two very important levels:

1. In the buying and selling of **outputs** (goods and services) through the use of **prices**;

2. In the buying and selling of **inputs** (land, labor, capital) through the use of **rent**, **wages**, and **interest** (the cost of borrowing money).

Why: The reason that the individual and the business voluntarily do business with each other—buying and selling inputs and outputs—is simple and logical: *They both expect to benefit.*

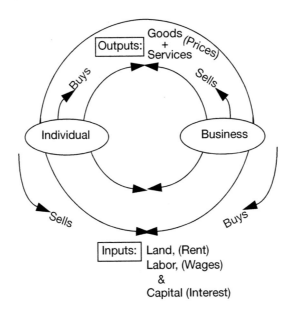

Personal Economics

On the lines below, try to explain the following transactions:

1. You (the buyer) and a business (the seller) came to a mutually beneficial agreement about the purchase of a particular good.

   The particular good: _____

   How this transaction was good for you, the buyer: _____

   _____

   How this transaction was good for a business, the seller: _____

   _____

2. Now, switch roles. Explain how you (the seller) and a business (the buyer) came to a mutually beneficial agreement about: 1) the use of your **labor** for a recent job; 2) the use of your **land** for a new bike shop; and 3) the use of your **capital** for the purchase of a new piece of equipment.

(continued)

Name_____ Date_____

◆ YOU AND THE BUSINESS DO BUSINESS . . . TWICE! ◆ *(continued)*

How these three transactions were good for you, the seller:

(a) Labor _____

(b) Land _____

(c) Capital _____

How these three transactions were good for a business, the buyer:

(a) Labor _____

(b) Land _____

(c) Capital _____

Beyond the Bottom Line

Take a look at a celebrity who is in the news today. Now, try to find some specific information about a deal that star has just signed with a business. For example, the actress Julia Roberts recently starred in the movie *Erin Brockovich* for $20 million. Los Angeles Laker center Shaquille O'Neal makes more than $17 million per season. These deals lead to debate over the star's whopping salary: "How can she possibly be worth that much? How can she make all this money and _____ make so much less? (Fill in the blank with your favorite underpaid occupation—I like teachers!) Your job is to pretend that you are the business that just signed a celebrity to a big contract. Now you must publicly justify this deal. Why does this deal make economic sense to your business? How does your business intend to make money on this deal? Be as specific, logical, and persuasive as possible. Consider all the usual criticisms. Respond to them as if you really were the head of a Hollywood studio or the owner of the Lakers!

Celebrity: _____

Special skills, talents, achievements: _____

_____

_____

Terms of deal: _____
(Cite source of information.)

Justification: _____

_____

_____

_____

(continued)

◆ YOU AND THE BUSINESS DO BUSINESS . . . TWICE! ◆ *(continued)*

 Internet Economics

The Web offers many examples of sellers wooing buyers, and occasionally buyers wooing sellers. Most examples involve goods and services (outputs), but some involve job opportunities, capital, and real estate (inputs).

We noted earlier that companies like Microsoft (**www.microsoft.com**) post job openings. Of course, they aren't the only companies looking to "buy" labor on the Net; lots of companies looking for qualified workers post electronic want ads on the Web.

Capital is also advertised on the Web. Banks, investment banks, and venture capital firms are in the business of providing capital to businesses. Check out Allied Capital, a venture capital firm based in Washington, D.C., at **www.alliedcapital.com**. It makes loans to small businesses, specifically for "start-up companies,

machinery and equipment purchases, real estate purchases and mortgage loans, and construction financings."

Commercial real estate is for sale all over the Web. For example, if you're in the market for a New York City office, you might like this ad for an office in New York's Rockefeller Center, recently advertised at **www.hia.com/rockctr**. "The perfect combination is a business address with worldwide recognition and the advantages inherent in a fully equipped and expertly staffed business center. You can have both in Rockefeller Center."

See if you can find one additional example (each) of land, labor, and capital "for sale" on the Web. List the correct Web addresses, and include a one-sentence summary of each input being offered for sale.

Land

Web address: _____

Summary: _____

Labor

Web address: _____

Summary: _____

Capital

Web address: _____

Summary: _____

                                       Activities for Economics Education

Activity 6
Money Makes the Economy Go 'Round!

Lesson Summary

Money, defined as any generally accepted medium of exchange, is *the* tool of any modern economy, since it makes transactions far easier than does barter.

Objectives

- Students will see firsthand that an economy without money functions only at a very basic level and with great difficulty. Students will also understand that money is valuable not for what it is, but for what it can buy.

Background

This activity builds on virtually all of the preceding activities. Money is the lubricant that enables the entire apparatus already introduced to run, to run smoothly, and to grow.

Materials

Name tags for all students

Directions

1. Have students read The Bottom Line and complete Personal Economics. Discuss.

2. Immediately commence Beyond the Bottom Line, following directions carefully. Allow approximately 10 minutes for Stage 1, 10 minutes for Stage 2, and 15 minutes for Stage 3. As indicated, record all valid transactions in Stages 1 and 2. Lead the analysis and discussion in Stage 3, but try to let the class draw the inevitable conclusion that money makes the economy function far more easily and better than barter.

3. Assign Internet Economics for homework.

Time Needed

1–2 class periods

Assessment and Evaluation

The Internet Economics homework should be checked to see if students were successful in finding three on-line companies that are in the business of money. Do students describe these businesses—and what they do—accurately? Do students understand how these businesses help the economy?

Further Applications

An opinion question that should provoke a most interesting discussion is, "Is money the root of all evil or the answer to all of our problems?"

 Web Sites

www.wiso.gwdg.de/ifbg/geld.html
www.wisbank.com

Name_____ Date_____

◆ MONEY MAKES THE ECONOMY GO 'ROUND! ◆

 ## *The Bottom Line*

One thing that is almost always needed in a transaction between a buyer and seller is **money**. Most countries create their own coins or currency for use as money. This is because money is easier than **barter**, or the direct exchange of two products, for the distribution of goods and services. In fact, if we had to depend on barter, we wouldn't be trading or producing much. We'd probably be spending most of our time just trying to survive from one day to the next. Money makes our economy work.

Personal Economics

Try to imagine what your life would be like if you had to barter to get the goods and services you need. Make a list of the essentials (food, utilities, shelter, etc.) you would have to get every month to live an adequate lifestyle. Now, summarize in writing the talents and skills you possess that could be directly traded for the goods and services you want.

Assess your situation. Do you think you could get everything you need just to survive?

The bare essentials: _____

_____

My talents and skills: _____

_____

Will I survive? _____

 ## *Beyond the Bottom Line*

Stage 1: A Barter (Moneyless) Society. Each individual in the class should choose a real-life profession, one that perhaps you would like to pursue when you finish school. Write your name and profession on a name tag, as in "Hi, I'm Kim, and I am a Lawyer."

Next, go out and mingle as you would at a party. Once you've had the chance to meet everyone, and more importantly see what they do—what skills or goods they offer—write down on a small sheet of paper what goods or services you would like to buy from your classmates. "I see that Joe makes sports cars and Terri owns a candy store. I want a new sports car and a lot of fudge."

Now, go among your classmates armed only with the skill or talent (practicing law) that you are willing to trade, or barter, for your desires (a new sports car and lots of fudge). Finding someone willing to barter—that is, they have something you want *and* you have something they want *and* both parties are willing to trade—is

called a **double coincidence of wants**. If such a coincidence happens, tell the teacher, who will record the terms of your exchange—for example, 1 hour of legal services for 10 pounds of fudge. Try to get everything you want on your list.

Stage 2: Add Money. Now, assume every person in the class just got $50,000 in cash. You may now offer either your skill—or money—to get what you want. If you find someone willing to make a transaction, tell the teacher, who will record the exchange. Try to get everything you want on your list.

Stage 3: Analysis. Which society—the barter or the money society—yielded more transactions?

_____

Why?_____

_____

Were you able to get what you wanted in the moneyless society?_____

Were you able to get what you wanted in the moneyed society?_____

(continued)

◆ MONEY MAKES THE ECONOMY GO 'ROUND! ◆ *(continued)*

Internet Economics

There is a terrific site (**www.wiso.gwdg.de/ifbg/geld.html**), sponsored by Göttingen University in Germany, that features some excellent information about money, its history and significance. The site also offers several pieces analyzing the changing form and role of money today, as people switch to cash cards, digital money, and electronic payment systems.

Banks play a critical role in the circulation of money. They accept it for safekeeping in the form of deposits. They lend out much of it both to people, for such things as car loans and mortgages, and to businesses that need additional capital. In essence, banks provide currency and other forms of money to consumers, and they serve as intermediaries between savers and borrowers. Several banks in Wisconsin have created their own web site (**www.wisbank.com**), where they advertise their services to consumers and businesses alike. Their web site contains specific information about personal finance, consumer trends, and ideas for entrepreneurs. The banks have also published some on-line

photos of bank robbers in the section entitled "Find a crook; get a reward"—a different kind of example of the power of money!

Find three other web sites that are in the business of money—corporations that handle or provide money for customers. List their web addresses. Summarize briefly who they are, what they do, and how they help the economy function and grow.

Web Site 1: _____

Summary: _____

_____

Web Site 2: _____

Summary: _____

_____

Web Site 3: _____

Summary: _____

_____

ACTIVITY 7
MARKETS AND PRICES RULE!

Lesson Summary

Money prices encourage the efficient production and allocation of all of the (scarce) goods and services that consumers demand. In theory, a price-driven free market should push the total number of products demanded by consumers to match *exactly* the total number of products supplied by producers.

Objectives

- Students will see firsthand that money, in the form of prices, does in fact make markets work, directly building on the last activity.

Materials

- small cards that you need to fill out beforehand for all students
- enough new pencils for at least half the class.

Directions

1. Have students read The Bottom Line and read and complete the Personal Economics exercise. The vital function served by prices is to make possible a transaction between the buyer and the seller.

2. Immediately commence the Beyond the Bottom Line, dividing the class equally into buyers and sellers. Prior to class, you should have filled out a confidential buy or sell card for each student in the following manner:

   To *all* buyers: Pay no more than $2.
   To *all* sellers: Sell for at least $1.

   Signal the opening of the pencil market with the expressed hope that all buyers and sellers can make a mutually beneficial transaction. Record all valid transactions, then close the market after about five minutes. Reopen the market and play a second round, then a third. Finally, lead the class in its analysis of the results.

   The point of this project is to have students see that prices make possible mutually advantageous transactions. Any buyers able to purchase a pencil for less than or equal to their maximum benefited. Any sellers able to sell for more than or equal to their minimum benefited. If you play several rounds of this game, you should also find that the transaction prices will move toward an equilibrium as people learn what others are

charging—and paying. Information and competition are powerful in a market environment. If I know what others are charging and paying and if I know other buyers and sellers are eager to take my place if I don't make the sale, then prices will move to a competitive equilibrium. Economically speaking, the equilibrium price is the price at which quantity demanded—that is, all of the buyers who wanted pencils—equals quantity supplied—that is, all of the sellers who wanted to sell pencils—and the market is cleared. See Activity 8.

3. Finally, assign Internet Economics, perhaps in preparation for commencing the long-term Stock Market project described in Appendix 1.

Time Needed

1–2 class periods

Assessment and Evaluation

You may evaluate individuals by their level of enthusiastic participation in the Beyond the Bottom Line.

Further Applications

You can manipulate the pricing cards so that some buyers and sellers do not, *cannot*, make deals. The point here is that, in these cases, buyers and sellers must be willing to reassess their price if they want to clinch a deal. In a free market, it's up to the buyer and the seller. If they want to make a deal, they can, but remember, a buyer or seller doesn't have to do anything he logically doesn't want to do, like lose money.

 Web Sites

www.nyse.com   www.quick-reilly.com
www.amex.com   www.dbc.com
www.nasdaq.com   www.hoovers.com
www.brokerlinks.com   www.wsj.com

◆ MARKETS AND PRICES RULE! ◆

 ## The Bottom Line

In a free market with money, prices rule. And what do they rule? Behavior. Consumer behavior. Producer behavior. Producers and consumers act—they sell and buy—when they both believe the price is right.

Prices provide information to consumers and producers that encourages the production and allocation of all the goods and services that consumers demand. In theory, a price-driven free market should push the total number of products

$10,000

demanded by consumers to exactly match the total number of products supplied by producers.

 ## Personal Economics

On the chart below, list five goods you would like to buy right now but can't afford. Write the estimated current market price next to each good you listed. Now, assume the market price for each good starts going down, or declining. Record the highest price you would be willing to pay for each good.

Good	Current Market Price	Highest Price You'd Pay
1.		
2.		
3.		
4.		
5.		

You can now buy each of the items you listed for your offered price. What vital function do you think prices have served in this exercise?

 ## Beyond the Bottom Line

Your teacher will divide the class into buyers and sellers of pencils. Each buyer gets a *confidential* pricing card dictating the highest price he or she is willing to pay for a fancy new pencil—such as, "Pay no more than $__ for a new pencil; if possible, pay less." Each seller gets a new pencil and a confidential pricing card dictating the lowest price he or she is willing to accept for that pencil—"Sell your pencil for at least $__; if possible, sell it for a higher price."

The teacher will signal when the pencil market opens. Prospective buyers and sellers meet to try to make a transaction at a mutually agreeable price. Report all successful transactions to your teacher. Play several rounds, and then discuss the results:

• Who was able to make a successful transaction?

• Did each party benefit from the transaction?

(continued)

◆ MARKETS AND PRICES RULE! ◆ *(continued)*

- Did some parties benefit more than others? Check the difference between the transaction price and the minimum/maximum price on the card. For instance, if I sold my pencil for $1.90 and my card said to sell for at least $1.00, then I realized an *additional* benefit/revenue of $0.90. If I bought my pencil for $1.45 and my card said to buy for no more than $2.00, then I realized an *additional* benefit of $0.55.

- What was the range of prices in Round 1? Round 2? Round 3?

- What do you conclude?

Internet Economics

The stock market is an excellent example of a market with many buyers and sellers whose behavior is ruled by prices. And this world-famous market can now be played, watched, and analyzed on the Net.

What is the stock market? Well, to be precise, there are three stock markets in the United States: the New York Stock Exchange (NYSE), the American Stock Exchange (AMEX), and the NASDAQ Market. The New York and American Stock Exchanges are located on or near Wall Street in New York City. The NASDAQ is "located" on a vast computer network linking brokers throughout the country. These world-famous stock markets have their own web sites at **www.nyse.com, www.amex.com**, and **www.nasdaq.com**. All three markets are sites where shares of stock, or certificates of ownership in companies, are bought and sold.

The Dow Jones Index is a market indicator that tracks the price movements of 30 of the largest and best-known company stocks. "The Dow" is the most widely quoted market index, though it is one of many indices and tracks only a small, though influential, segment of the overall stock market.

Buying and selling stock has gotten so easy for the average investor that you can now do it over the Internet! **Www.brokerlinks.com** lists brokerage firms that allow you to start your trade—for a fee, called a **commission**—over the Internet. One well-known on-line discount brokerage house is Quick and Reilly (**www.quick-reilly.com**), which will execute your buy/sell order once you have set up an account.

While on-line trading promises even faster execution than the "call up your broker" system, the process is basically the same. And the bottom line is unchanged. For my IBM stock to sell, someone must want to buy my shares at a mutually agreeable price. Price plays the key role in bringing buyers and sellers together, since buy orders must match sell orders.

To watch the stock market in action over the Internet, check out **www.dbc.com**. This site tracks stock prices for individual companies, as well as overall market movement throughout the day.

To research individual company stocks to learn whether you want to buy or sell them, check out **www.hoovers.com** or **www.wsj.com**. For a fee, these sites will analyze the company stock you are interested in. An increasing number of companies have produced their own web sites, offering information about their products, services, management, objectives, and so forth.

Find three more web sites that deal with the stock market. List their Web addresses, and give a brief summary of what each site offers.

Web site 1: _____

Web address: _____

Summary: _____

Web site 2: _____

Web address: _____

Summary: _____

Web site 3: _____

Web address: _____

Summary: _____

ACTIVITY 8
DEMAND AND SUPPLY: THE MEANING

Lesson Summary

Demand represents consumer intent to *buy* a good or service at a certain range of prices.
Supply represents producer intent to *sell* a good or service at a certain range of prices.
As price increases, consumers typically desire fewer units of a good or service
while producers make more units available; as price decreases, the reverse happens.

Objectives

- Students will see for themselves—through plotting points, drawing curves, and explaining in their own words—that demand and supply are two uniquely separate perspectives, the consumer's and the producer's, with different definitions, laws, and graphs.

Background

While demand and supply do come together in the next activity, it's crucial that students not mix them (up) now.

Directions

1. Have students read the Demand section, starting with The Bottom Line. Make certain they clearly understand the concepts described. Ask students for other concrete examples of demand in action.

2. Have students read and complete Personal Economics (Demand) and Beyond the Bottom Line (Demand), which ask for a simple graph and a straightforward explanation, respectively, of consumer demand.

3. Then have students read the Supply section, starting with The Bottom Line. Make certain they clearly understand the concepts described. Ask students for other concrete examples of supply in action.

4. Assign for homework Personal Economics (Supply) and Beyond the Bottom Line

(Supply), which again ask for a simple graph and a straightforward explanation, respectively, this time of producer supply.

5. Also assign as homework Internet Economics, which will give students an additional opportunity to discover examples of demand and supply in action and prompt students to find other web sites devoted to the explanation and illustration of these concepts.

Time Needed

2 class periods

Assessment and Evaluation

Look over students' completed Personal Economics and Beyond the Bottom Line for both demand and supply to see if they drew their curves correctly and explained the laws of demand and supply clearly. Collect Internet Economics to see if they found another demand and supply web site and summarized the information accurately.

Further Applications

Consider other goods, make up realistic numbers (dollars and units), plot points, draw curves, and discuss—but keep demand and supply separate.

 Web Sites

www.usgs.gov
www.huntforpro.com

◆ DEMAND AND SUPPLY: THE MEANING ◆

Demand

 ### *The Bottom Line*

What is **demand**? Demand represents consumers' intent to buy something at a certain range of prices. As price increases, consumers typically desire fewer units of a good or service. As price decreases, consumers typically desire more units of that good or service. Demand, of course, can also apply to business demand—for land, labor, and capital. The same rules, schedules, and curves apply.

Personal Economics

Let's say I want to buy one delicious red apple if it is priced at $1. I'll buy two apples if the price is 75 cents each, and three apples if they are selling at 50 cents each. Why would I want to do that? The answer goes back to logical decision making. If the price of a good I want declines, then I can increase my net value (benefit-cost) by buying more. Check the difference between purchasing two apples and three apples. My cost ($1.50) stays the same. My benefit increases (three apples bought vs. two). As a result, my net value increases, too. Draw the graph for the Demand for Red Apples on the grid by plotting the three points given: one apple at $1, two apples at $0.75, and three apples at $0.50.

Now, connect the dots. What do you have? You have a downward-sloping **demand curve**. Label this curve D

for demand. This is a significant result. Nearly all demand curves slope down, because most people are logical about their purchases. As the price of a good consumers want declines, then the quantity of that good demanded will increase.

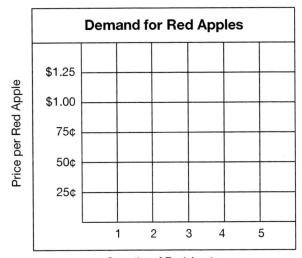

Quantity of Red Apples

This is true for one person who wants to buy red apples; it is even truer for all consumers of red apples. I may not want more than three apples. However, red apple consumers *as a whole* want to buy many more apples as the price declines. The consumer demand curve for red apples looks different than my individual demand curve. But they both share the same important property: *They both slope down to the right*. Individual consumers and consumers as a whole usually act rationally. This means they love lower prices and want to buy more as prices go down.

(continued)

25   *Activities for Economics Education*

Name_____ Date _____

 ## *Beyond the Bottom Line*

We have established the **law of demand**: As price (*P*) declines, quantity demanded (*Qd*) increases. The law of demand also states that as price (*P*) increases, quantity demanded (*Qd*) decreases. Can you explain why in your own words?

As price increases, quantity demanded decreases, because _____

_____

Supply

 ## *The Bottom Line*

What is **supply**? Supply represents producers' intent to sell something at a certain range of prices. As price increases, producers typically make more units of their good or service available; as price decreases, producers typically make fewer units of their good or service available. Supply can also apply to individual supply—of land, labor, and capital. The same rules, schedules, and curves apply.

 ## *Personal Economics*

The Red Apple Farming Company is willing and able to sell 100 apples at $1 each. They will sell 200 apples at $2 each, and 300 apples at $3 each. Why? The answer once again is based on logical decision making. If the price of a good/service a company wants to sell increases, then the company can increase its **revenue** (price times quantity) and thus its **profit** (revenue minus cost).

Look at the difference between selling 200 apples and 300 apples. Red Apple Farming can increase its revenue by $500. And if costs don't change at all, then Red Apple Farming's profits increase by $500, too, since revenue grew by $500 and costs increased by $0. In fact, even if costs increase somewhat, the company will still increase its profits. Thus, there is a powerful incentive for companies to increase production if prices rise.

Draw the graph for the Red Apple Farming Company on the grid below by plotting the three points given: 100 apples at $1, 200 apples at $2, and 300 apples at $3.

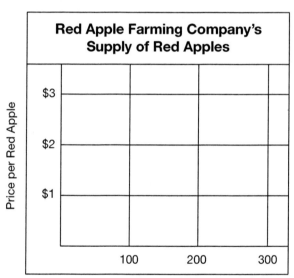

Red Apple Farming Company's Supply of Red Apples

Price per Red Apple / Quantity of Red Apples

Now, connect the dots. What do you have? You have an upward-sloping **supply curve**. Label this curve *S* for supply. This is also a significant result. Nearly all supply curves slope up, because most companies are logical about their sales. As the price of a good increases, then the quantity supplied of that good will also increase.

(continued)

◆ DEMAND AND SUPPLY: THE MEANING ◆ *(continued)*

This is true for the Red Apple Farming Company; it is even truer for *all* producers of red apples. Red Apple may not want to produce more than 300 apples (maybe they only have one acre of land set aside for apple trees); for this reason, their supply curve ends at 300 (*x* coordinate), $3.00 (*y* coordinate). On the other hand, red apple producers *as a whole* probably want to sell many more apples at higher and higher prices. The producer supply curve for red apples looks different from Red Apple's individual supply curve, but they both share the same crucial property: *They both slope up to the right*. Individual companies and producers as a whole usually act rationally: They love higher prices and profits and want to sell more!

Beyond the Bottom Line

We have established the **law of supply**: As price *(P)* increases, quantity supplied *(Qs)* increases. The law of supply also states that as price *(P)* decreases, quantity supplied *(Qs)* decreases. Can you explain why in your own words?

As price increases, quantity supplied increases because _____

_____

Internet Economics

The real fun in demand and supply curves comes when you put them together. In the meantime, some web sites refer to supply and demand as separate entities—the best way to learn them.

At **www.usgs.gov**, the United States Geological Survey, a government agency, offers "statistics and information on the worldwide supply, demand, and flow of minerals and materials essential to the U.S. economy, the national security, and protection of the environment."

Hunt Forest Products, Inc. (**www. huntforpro.com**), based in Ruston, Louisiana, is involved in supply *and* demand. The company sells plywood, veneer, and lumber products (supply) but also "is in the market to buy land and timber" (demand).

Check out some of the more academic web sites, often posted by professors and graduate students, for another look at how supply and demand are explained and illustrated. Search under "demand" or "supply" or "economics" or a related word. Note a particularly good site, with address, that you found. Summarize in writing what you learned.

Web site: _____

Web address: _____

_____

Summary: _____

_____

_____

_____

ACTIVITY 9
DEMAND AND SUPPLY: THE MEETING

Lesson Summary

Demand and supply curves, which reflect distinct consumer and producer intentions, intersect at an **equilibrium price** (*Pe*), where consumers want a certain number of, for example, delicious red apples (quantity demanded, or *Qd*) and producers are willing to supply exactly that number (quantity supplied, or *Qs*). If the going **market price** (*MP*) is equal to the equilibrium price (*Pe*), then a most efficient state has been reached: *Qd=Qs*. But in those situations where the market price is either above or below the equilibrium price, a **shortage** (*Qd>Qs*) or **surplus** (*Qs>Qd*) of apples develops.

Objectives

- Students will see firsthand that demand and supply for a given good or service take on great significance when they are analyzed together, especially on a graph.

Background

Intersecting demand and supply curves and knowledge of the market price can illustrate a satisfying market equilibrium or a frustrating disequilibrium.

Directions

1. Have students read The Bottom Line. The key point to stress is that if consumer and producer intentions match—that is, buyers are eager to buy and sellers to sell over the same range of prices—then demand and supply curves will intersect on a graph and a price and quantity equilibrium can be found.

2. This important concept should become clearer as students read and complete Personal Economics. The answers to questions in this section follow: 1. 2,000; 2. Apple producers will try to eliminate the surplus of apples (inventory) by reducing their price; 3. At $0.50, there is a shortage (*Qd>Qs*) of 1,000 apples as consumers fight to get their hands on 3,000 apples but only 2,000 are made available by producers. There will be significant pressure to raise the price to $1, the equilibrium, market-clearing price, where quantity demanded equals quantity supplied.

3. Go over Beyond the Bottom Line—A Graphical Review, since it's the clearest and easiest way for students to understand and retain these concepts.

4. Assign Internet Economics for homework. Make sure students understand why the supply curve in the case of arena or stadium tickets is usually vertical since the number of seats is fixed.

Time Needed

2–3 class periods

Assessment and Evaluation

For Internet Economics, evaluate how realistically and accurately students derive and draw demand and supply curves for the chosen event. Assess analysis. If there's a shortage of tickets, the arena or promoter should raise prices (scalpers perform the same function!); if there's a surplus, the arena or promoter should lower prices.

Further Applications

It's fun and helpful to devise as many additional real-life demand and supply scenarios as time permits.

 **Web Sites**

www.ticketmaster.com

◆ DEMAND AND SUPPLY: THE MEETING ◆

The Bottom Line

A transaction takes place when demand and supply intersect. That happens at an **equilibrium price** (*Pe*), where consumers want a certain number of an item (**quantity demanded**, or *Qd*) and producers are willing to supply exactly that number (**quantity supplied**, or *Qs*). No producer or consumer willing to deal at that market price goes home unhappy. But in those situations where the market price (*MP*) is either above or below the equilibrium price (*Pe*), a **shortage** (*Qd>Qs*) or **surplus** (*Qs>Qd*) of the item develops.

It's not that difficult to see what happens when demand and supply meet, especially using a graph.

Personal Economics

Here is the overall consumer demand schedule for red apples, calculated from the individual demand schedules of many consumers, including me:

Price (*P*)	Quantity Demanded (*Qd*)
$5.00	0
$2.50	1,000
$2.00	1,500
$1.50	2,000
$1.00	2,500
$0.50	3,000
$0.10	5,000

This overall producer supply schedule for red apples has been calculated from the individual supply schedules of many producers:

Price (*P*)	Quantity Supplied (*Qs*)
$5.00	5,000
$2.50	4,000
$2.00	3,500
$1.50	3,000
$1.00	2,500
$0.50	2,000
$0.10	0

Graph both schedules on the grid below. Be sure to label your curves *D* and *S*.

Red Apples

Price per Red Apple

$5.00
$4.00
$3.00
$2.00
$1.00

1000 2000 3000 4000 5000

Quantity of Red Apples

(continued)

Name_____ Date_____

◆ DEMAND AND SUPPLY: THE MEETING ◆ (continued)

Analyze the supply and demand schedules, the resulting curves, and the graph you produced. At what price does the quantity of red apples demanded (Qd) equal the quantity of red apples supplied (Qs)? _____

The answer should be clear to you. At $1 per apple, consumers want to buy 2,500 apples and producers are willing to sell 2,500 apples. Label this point X at the place where the demand and supply curves intersect. The equilibrium price (Pe) is $1, and 2,500 is the equilibrium quantity (Qe, where Qd=Qs). At this special price, the market is cleared. At Pe, no consumers ready to buy apples for $1 go home empty-handed. No producers willing to sell apples for $1 don't sell their entire stock.

But only $1 works as the equilibrium price. Skeptical? Good! Let's prove it by trying other prices, like $2. There are lots of buyers and sellers at that price, right? Well, let's take a look at the supply and demand schedules and at the graph itself.

At a market price (MP) of $2, consumers are demanding 1,500 red apples. Producers are supplying 3,500 red apples. That makes sense, doesn't it? More producers find $2 attractive, but that price repels more consumers than a $1 price. Do you see the unfortunate result?

1. What is the surplus (Qs>Qd) of apples not being sold? _____

_____

You can see this from the graph. Draw a dotted line horizontally from the y axis at $2 all the way across the graph. The dotted line intersects the demand curve first (at x=1,500 and y=$2). Further along, it intersects the supply curve (at x=3,500 and y=$2). The gap between the two points is the apple surplus, and it's a big problem for apple producers.

2. What are they going to do with all those unsold, soon-to-rot apples, also known as their inventory? _____

_____

If you're still skeptical about $1 as the price equilibrium, let's look at another price, this time below the equilibrium—$0.50. What's going to happen there?

3. Study the supply and demand schedules and draw in another dotted line across the graph at y=$0.50. Now explain in your own words what will happen at this price.

_____

_____

🖾 *Beyond the Bottom Line—A Graphical Review*

It's easiest to understand the meeting of supply and demand and to grasp the concepts of equilibrium, market price, surplus, and shortage by learning the following three graphs. In these graphs, the x axis (horizontal) equals the quantity. The y axis (vertical) equals the price. The S curve is the supply curve. The D curve is the demand curve:

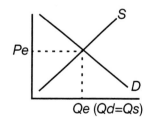

1. At Pe, Qe (Qd=Qs)
"The market clears"

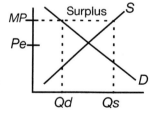

2. At MP above Pe, Qs>Qd
"Surplus"

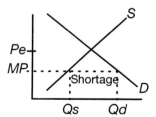

3. At MP below Pe, Qd>Qs
"Shortage"

30   *Activities for Economics Education*

(continued)

◆ DEMAND AND SUPPLY: THE MEETING ◆ *(continued)*

Internet Economics

While it's tough to find actual supply and demand schedules and curves on the Net (apart from academic web sites), it's easy to find markets where producer supply and consumer demand come together.

One of the more interesting examples of demand meeting supply on the Net is the sale of concert and sporting events tickets on the Web. At **www.ticketmaster.com**, tickets to basketball games, concerts, and a variety of other events are made available to anyone with a valid credit card. Shopping for sports or concert tickets is just like shopping for any other good or service, with one crucial difference. The supply curve for a Madonna concert or a Knicks' basketball game at Madison Square Garden is *fixed*—a straight line up and down at a quantity of 20,000 seats—since the producer will offer no more and no less than 20,000 seats at *any* price. Why? Because the producer can't supply more seats without renovating the Garden or building a new arena or bribing the New York City fire marshal. Those options are time-consuming, expensive, or illegal.

With that in mind, link up with **www.ticketmaster.com** to see what event you would like to attend at any major arena in the country.

On a separate sheet of paper, complete the following four tasks:

1. Give a brief description of the event (concert/athletic contest, date, venue, etc.).

2. Estimate the popularity of this event. Produce a realistic demand schedule and curve for tickets at the arena that is hosting this event. Assume that all seats are sold at the same price, whether you're in the front row or the last row. Label all axes, curves, title, etc.

3. Find out the arena's seating capacity through Ticketmaster or through the arena's own web site. Produce a supply curve, which is vertical, for tickets. Label all axes, curves, title, etc.

4. Produce a new graph with supply and demand meeting. Label all axes, curves, title, etc.

Then answer the following four questions:

1. Analyze the intersection of *S* and *D*. What is the equilibrium price (*Pe*)? _____

2. How many tickets will be demanded (*Qd*) and sold (*Qs*) at *Pe*? _____

   Is *Pe* lower, higher, or equal to the market price (*MP*) that the arena is supposedly charging for

   all tickets? _____

3. Will a surplus or a shortage of tickets develop? _____

4. What do you recommend that the promoters of the concert/arena management do? _____

   _____

   _____

DEMAND AND SUPPLY: DYNAMIC, NOT STATIC

Lesson Summary

Demand (*D*) and supply (*S*)—the schedules and the curves themselves—shift in response to specific changes in outside factors. Consumer preferences, numbers, income, and prices of substitute goods affect demand while producer costs, technology, numbers, and alternative profit opportunities affect supply. As a result, when demand and/or supply shift, price and quantity equilibriums change, too.

Objectives

- Students will see demand and supply as more that just dry definitions, amounts and prices on a schedule, or curves on a graph. They will recognize that demand and supply represent real intentions and actions, and that as a result, they are *dynamic*, not static, phenomena.

Materials

- different colored chalk to use for each new *D* or *S* curve

Directions

1. Have students read Changes in Demand, starting with The Bottom Line. Make sure they understand *why* demand—the schedule and the curve—changes and what happens *when* demand changes (the *D* curve shifts). You may also wish to explain in more detail the distinction between a change in supply and a change in quantity supplied (*Qs*).

2. Students should read and complete Personal Economics, which asks them to graph a new *D* curve (for red apples) that has shifted to the right of the old *D* curve because of a change in consumer preferences.

3. Once students have completed their graphs, immediately commence Beyond the Bottom Line. This activity asks groups of students to construct realistic *D* schedules and curves (on paper and then on the classroom chalkboard) for the CDs of a formerly hot musical group to show how *D* has shifted to reflect the band's rise and fall.

4. Have students read Changes in Supply, starting with The Bottom Line. Make sure they understand why supply—the schedule and the curve—changes and what happens *when* it changes.

5. Beyond the Bottom Line, which can be assigned for homework, asks students to produce another graph illustrating shifting *D* and *S* curves and the resulting effect on equilibrium price (*Pe*) and quantity (*Qe*). Students should answer the questions posed.

6. Also assign Internet Economics for homework. If students are confused about the assignment, offer problems from Further Applications as examples.

Time Needed

1–2 class periods

(continued)

Assessment and Evaluation

The list below provides answers to Beyond the Bottom Line questions:

1. *Pe*=$1; *Qe* (*Qd*=*Qs*) is 2,500 apples.

2. *Pe2*=$2.50; *Qe2* (*Qd2*=*Qs2*) is 2,000 apples

3. Supply has decreased, thus shifting the *S* curve to the left; demand has increased, thus shifting the *D* curve to the right. The resulting equilibriums, noted in answer 2, make sense because price has clearly increased due to stronger consumer preference for a good that is less available than it was before, which also explains the decline in the number sold. Despite the increase in popularity, some people balked at paying the higher price.

Check Internet Economics homework to see if students clearly understand the concept of shifting demand and supply curves.

Further Applications

You can ask students to explain some real-life price changes using (shifting) supply and demand curves.

1. Prices of color TVs have dropped from about $2,000 in 1960 to about $250 today, despite increasing sales and the fact that today's sets boast much better quality and many more features. (*S* shifts right.)

2. Prices of LP records have dropped from about $10.98 in 1983 to $1.98 in 1997. (*D* shifts left.)

3. The price of gasoline jumped from $.30 per gallon in 1972 to $1.00 in 1974, after some oil-producing countries cut gas exports to the U.S. (*S* shifts left.)

 Web Sites

www.washingtonpost.com
www.latimes.com

Name_____ Date_____

◆ DEMAND AND SUPPLY: DYNAMIC, NOT STATIC ◆

Changes in Demand

💰 *The Bottom Line*

Does demand change? About as often as we change our minds—in other words, yes! A lot!

There are four things that would cause a change in demand:

1. Changes in consumer preference

2. Changes in consumer incomes

3. Changes in the prices of related goods or services, known as **substitutes**

4. Changes in the number of consumers in the market

Any of these changes can signal a surge in popularity for a particular good or service at any given price; this will cause a rightward shift in the demand curve. Alternatively, these changes can signal a loss of popularity for a particular good or service. This will cause a leftward shift in the demand curve. Note that a change in price alone does not cause a change in demand; it causes a change in **quantity demanded (Qd)** and a movement along the demand curve.

🖩 *Personal Economics*

Remember the overall consumer demand schedule and accompanying curve for red apples? Let's say that consumer preferences, including mine, have changed. A new scientific study links apple consumption with a healthier life ("An apple a day . . ."). Because of this, consumers now want more red apples at any given price. Check out how many apples consumers wanted at $1 before the study came out (2,500) and how many they want now (3,500)! The change in preference is evident at every given price. Where before apples were selling x units at a given price, now they're selling $x+1,000$ units. See for yourself:

DEMAND SCHEDULE FOR RED APPLES

	Before Study	**After Study**
P	**Qd**	**Qd**
$5.00	0	1,000
$2.50	1,000	2,000
$2.00	1,500	2,500
$1.50	2,000	3,000
$1.00	2,500	3,500
$0.50	3,000	4,000
$0.10	5,000	6,000

Draw one graph including both the old (before scientific study) demand curve and the new (after scientific study) demand curve. Label properly and thoroughly. Make sure you distinguish between the two demand curves. For example, use D_1 for the old demand curve and D_2 for the new one. *Note:* Shifts are not always parallel like this!

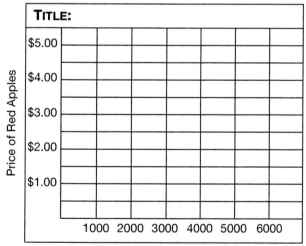

TITLE:

(Price of Red Apples: $5.00, $4.00, $3.00, $2.00, $1.00)
(Quantity of Red Apples: 1000 2000 3000 4000 5000 6000)

(continued)

◆ DEMAND AND SUPPLY: DYNAMIC, NOT STATIC ◆ *(continued)*

What has happened? Because of a change in consumer preferences, demand—the curve and the schedule it represents—has changed. (Of course, it still naturally follows the law of demand and slopes downward.) More specifically, demand has *increased* and its curve has shifted to the *right*. Apples are suddenly more popular at every given price. The new demand curve (D_2) reflects that.

What would happen if apples instead became less popular, as news of a massive worm infestation reached consumers? At any given price, Qd (the number of apples demanded) would decline. This would change the entire demand schedule and shift an even newer demand curve (D_2) to the left.

Demand has declined. Draw D_3 on the graph on page 34.

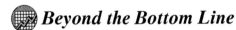

Beyond the Bottom Line

What in the world does pop music have to do with shifting demand curves? Answer: A lot!

The Rise and Fall of a Rock Band

Assume three stages of popularity in the life of a once-popular rock music group, like _____ (pick one!):

- Stage I: modest popularity (a relatively unknown band)

- Stage II: tremendous popularity (platinum CD time!)

- Stage III: washed-up popularity (yesterday's sound)

The teacher will divide the class into three groups. Each group is responsible for charting the relative success (how many CDs sold at several possible prices) of a rock group at one stage. Each group will be given one price/quantity combination. The group is to figure out other realistic price/quantity combinations and graph their stage's demand curve.

- Stage I Group: The band sells 200,000 CDs at $14.95 per CD. How many CDs would they sell at $13.95? $15.95? Other prices? Produce a demand schedule/chart and a corresponding graph of your demand curve with proper labels, axes, etc.

- Stage II Group: The band sells 1,000,000 CDs at $14.95 per CD. How many CDs would they sell at $13.95? $15.95? Other prices? Produce a demand schedule/chart and a corresponding graph of your demand curve with proper labels, axes, etc.

- Stage III Group: The band sells 10,000 CDs at $14.95 per CD. How many CDs would they sell at $13.95? $15.95? Other prices? Produce a demand schedule/chart and a corresponding graph of your demand curve with proper labels, axes, etc.

When your group is ready to show your data to the teacher, choose one representative to graph your stage's demand curve on one large common graph on the chalkboard. (Use different colored chalk for each *D* curve, if possible). When all three groups have finished putting their demand curves on the large graph, each group should pick another representative to explain what the group's demand curve means. As a class, assess the shifting curves. What lessons can you draw from this exercise?

(continued)

◆ DEMAND AND SUPPLY: DYNAMIC, NOT STATIC ◆ *(continued)*

Changes in Supply

 The Bottom Line

What factors are behind shifts in supply—both the schedule and the curve—which can also change quickly and often?

1. Changes in the costs of production

2. Changes in technology used to make the good or service

3. Changes in profit opportunities available to producers by selling other goods and services

4. Changes in the number of sellers in the market

The bottom line with any of these changes is that each can signal one of two things: greater or easier (or cheaper) production at any given price, or diminished or more difficult (or more expensive) production. Greater (or easier or cheaper) production will cause a shift to the right in the supply curve. Diminished (or more difficult or more expensive) production will cause a shift to the left in the supply curve. Note that a change in price alone does not cause a change in supply; it causes a change in **quantity supplied** (*Qs*) and a movement along the supply curve.

 Beyond the Bottom Line

Putting it all together, the new supply and new demand curves meet again, but this time somewhere new. The result of all this curve-shifting, mind-changing, production-increasing or decreasing behavior is a new equilibrium price (Pe_2) and equilibrium quantity (Qe_2 where $Qd_2=Qs_2$). And where is that? Simple. Where the new Demand curve intersects the new Supply curve. Let's use our red apple example one last time. Here are the consumer data for the old (D_1) and new (D_2) demand schedules. The chart also lists the producer data for the old (S_1) and new (S_2) supply schedules. Put all four curves, with the proper labels, on the graph on page 37.

RED APPLES

	Supply Schedule		Demand Schedule	
	Before Wage Increase	After Wage Increase	Before Study	After Study
P	*Qs*	*Qs*	*Qd*	*Qd*
$5.00	5,000	3,000	0	1,000
$2.50	4,000	2,000	1,000	2,000
$2.00	3,500	1,500	1,500	2,500
$1.50	3,000	1,000	2,000	3,000
$1.00	2,500	500	2,500	3,500
$0.50	2,000	0	3,000	4,000
$0.10	0	0	5,000	6,000

(continued)

 Activities for Economics Education

◆ DEMAND AND SUPPLY: DYNAMIC, NOT STATIC ◆ (continued)

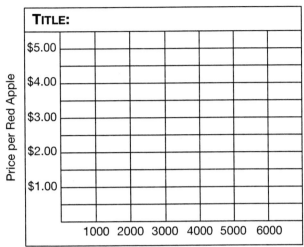

TITLE: _____

Price per Red Apple

$5.00

$4.00

$3.00

$2.00

$1.00

1000 2000 3000 4000 5000 6000

Quantity of Red Apples

1. What was the original price/quantity equilibrium (where S_1 and D_1 intersected)?

   _____

   _____

2. What is the new price/quantity equilibrium (where S_2 and D_2 intersect)?

   _____

   _____

3. In plain English, what has happened?

   _____

   _____

   _____

   _____

   _____

   _____

   _____

🖥️ Internet Economics

Recently, an article on changes in the price of California wines was found in *The Los Angeles Times* (**www.latimes.com**). The article laid the responsibility for higher wine prices on two factors. The first was an increased consumer preference for California wines (demand curve shifts right). The second reason was a rainy growing season that hurt the grape harvest in northern California (supply curve shifts left). The result was higher prices for California wines.

Find two other articles in on-line news reports about product price changes that can be explained/analyzed by shifts in demand and/or supply. Use graphs to illustrate them.

Article topic 1: _____

Web address: _____

Shift in supply/demand: _____

_____

Article topic 2: _____

Web address: _____

Shift in supply/demand: _____

_____

                                       Activities for Economics Education

ACTIVITY 11

DIFFERENT KINDS OF MARKETS: FROM COMPETITION TO MONOPOLY

Lesson Summary

The number of producers, or sellers, in a given market has a significant impact on a product's price and quantity (bought and sold). The four types of sellers' markets are monopoly, oligopoly, monopolistic competition, and perfect competition, with monopoly featuring the highest relative product prices and fewest quantities available and perfect competition boasting the opposite.

Objectives

- Students will recognize and describe the different market structures and experience for themselves the impact the number of sellers has on the relative prices and available quantities of a given good or service.

Materials

- note cards for the producers in Beyond the Bottom Line, filled out by you beforehand, that list the product to be sold and its cost of production

- play money

Directions

1. Have students read The Bottom Line and read and complete Personal Economics. Are the real-life examples of different sellers' markets cited by students accurate? (Monopoly and Perfect Competition are the two rarest markets.)

2. Immediately commence Beyond the Bottom Line. Assign students to fill various roles; follow the directions carefully. Stress to consumers that each person must buy at least one unit each of food, shelter, and clothing in order to survive; then, and only then, can they buy chocolate or formal wear or a tropical vacation! Stress to producers that they should try to maximize profits, but they are not permitted to talk to each other and set prices. Note successful transactions, recording transaction prices and producer profits reported by students, in both rounds. Lead the class in its post-game analysis. Students should see for themselves that as the number of producers increases, prices decline and the quantity of goods bought and sold increases. They should conclude that competition helps consumers but hurts producers, since their profits will erode as more competitors enter the market.

3. Assign Internet Economics for homework. After students have researched some web sites, ask them either to write an essay expressing their opinions or merely to come to class ready to offer and debate them.

Time Needed

1–2 class periods

Assessment and Evaluation

As noted, the Internet Economics assignment can take the form of an essay, which can be evaluated on the basis of clarity, thoroughness, and persuasiveness.

Further Applications

Are there some instances where monopolists benefit society? Inventors have a monopoly over their own inventions that could help society.

 Web Sites

www.essential.org/antitrust/microsoft

Name_____ Date_____

◆ DIFFERENT KINDS OF MARKETS: FROM COMPETITION TO MONOPOLY ◆

 ### *The Bottom Line*

Market size can be defined as the number of buyers and sellers in a given industry. It makes a big difference in a product's relative price and quantity (bought and sold). This is particularly true for sellers/producers. More competitive markets—markets where there are more sellers— offer lower product prices and greater quantities available than less competitive markets— markets where there are fewer sellers.

The different sellers' markets are characterized as follows:

1. A **monopoly** is a market ruled by a single seller who makes a product that has very few close competitors.

2. An **oligopoly** is a market where a small number of sellers make a good or service with a few close competitors.

3. **Monopolistic competition** is a market where there are many sellers making slightly different products.

4. **Perfect competition** is a market where there are a very large number of producers selling exactly the same product in large quantities at the lowest prices possible.

The one buyers' market worth mentioning is a **monopsony**, the relatively rare market characterized by a single buyer.

 ### *Personal Economics*

List some real-life examples of different sellers' markets you've seen or heard about.

1. Monopoly _____

2. Oligopoly _____

3. Monopolistic competition _____

4. Perfect competition _____

Which of the four markets do you think is most common? Why? _____

_____

_____

_____

Which of the four markets do you think is least common? Why? _____

_____

_____

_____

_____

(continued)

39   *Activities for Economics Education*

◆ DIFFERENT KINDS OF MARKETS:
FROM COMPETITION TO MONOPOLY ◆ *(continued)*

 Beyond the Bottom Line

Round 1

The class is divided into producers (six) and consumers (everybody else).

Each producer has a job and a product to sell, with cost of production noted.

Producer Job	Product	$ Cost of Production
1 farmer	Food	1
1 real estate developer	Shelter	100
1 seamstress	Clothing	10
1 chocolatier	Chocolate candies	1
1 resort operator	Tropical vacation	100
1 fashion designer	Formal wear	10

Each consumer gets $1,000 in play money and the following warning: "You must buy at least one unit of food, one unit of shelter, and one unit of clothing before the round ends, or you will die." Consumers may buy anything else they want if they have money and time remaining.

Producers are free to set/negotiate any price they want. Naturally, their objective is to maximize profits (revenue minus cost). No collusion (talking) between producers allowed!

Report all successful transactions (include price) to the teacher. At the end of the round, each producer should calculate and report his/her profits.

Round 2

The jobs of chocolatier, resort operator, and fashion designer are hereby eliminated. These people have become farmers, real estate developers, and seamstresses, so now there are two of each of those.

Producer Job	Product	$ Cost of Production
2 farmers	Food	1
2 real estate developers	Shelter	100
2 seamstresses	Clothing	10

Once again, each consumer gets $1,000 and the same survival warning.

Producers are to maximize profits, but no collusion permitted!

Report all successful transactions (include price) to the teacher. At the end of the round, each producer should calculate and report his/her profits.

(continued)

◆ DIFFERENT KINDS OF MARKETS:
FROM COMPETITION TO MONOPOLY ◆ *(continued)*

Post-game Analysis

1. What was the range of prices paid for food, shelter, and clothing in Round 1? _____

   _____

2. What was the range of prices paid for chocolate, a tropical vacation, and formal wear in

   Round 1? _____

3. What conclusion do you make about the price differences between essential and nonessential

   goods? _____

   _____

4. What was the range of prices paid for food, shelter, and clothing in Round 2? _____

   _____

5. What conclusion do you make about the effect of competition (in other words, additional

   producers) on market prices? _____

   _____

6. What was the range of profits reported by producers of food, shelter, and clothing

   in Round 1? _____

   in Round 2? _____

7. What conclusion do you make about the effect of competition (additional producers) on

   producer profits? _____

   _____

(continued)

◆ DIFFERENT KINDS OF MARKETS:
FROM COMPETITION TO MONOPOLY ◆ *(continued)*

 *Internet Economics*

Many web sites analyze and critique specific sellers' markets, like the so-called media and health oligopolies or Microsoft's alleged dominance of the computer software industry. In fact, the U.S. government's case against Microsoft has been the subject of a lot of web sites, as well as a lot of news articles. For news summaries, opinions, and legal documents, visit **www.essential.org/antitrust/microsoft**.

Where do you stand on the issue of government regulation of monopolies? Do you believe that monopoly behavior needs to be restrained or eliminated? Or do you believe that when it comes to monopolies, government is part of the problem? Check out additional sites and opinions on the Web and make up your own mind. Find at least three web sites that address the subject. List each web address, and summarize what you found on each site.

Web site 1: _____

Web address: _____

_____

Summary: _____

_____

_____

Web site 2: _____

Web address: _____

_____

Summary: _____

_____

_____

Web site 3: _____

Web address: _____

_____

Summary: _____

_____

_____

ACTIVITY 12
SAVINGS AND BANKS, A KEY ECONOMIC INSTITUTION

Lesson Summary

Banks play the middleman between savers and borrowers, paying interest to savers for their deposits and lending out most of those deposits—and charging a higher rate of interest— to borrowers (individuals or businesses) that need the money.

Objectives

- Students will understand the key role that banks play in the growth of the economy and see how they compete with each other for customers— depositors and borrowers—as they determine interest rates.

Materials

- a copy of Appendix II (pp. 84–85) for each student

Directions

1. Have students read The Bottom Line. If students have questions about the Federal Reserve, refer to Activity 18. Emphasize the key lending role that banks play in our economy, enabling individuals and businesses to buy or do things they otherwise could not afford, like purchase a car or build a new factory.

2. Skip Personal Economics for now, but assign it for homework; students are asked to call banks to find out what kinds of services they offer to depositors and borrowers.

3. Have students read, complete, and discuss Appendix II, "Finally, Understanding Interest and Interest Rates," before commencing Beyond the Bottom Line. Explain to students beforehand that depositors who keep more money in the bank longer with fewer cash withdrawals are paid a higher rate of interest because the banks are better able to lend out most of that money to a borrower; students should also know that borrowers who seem less likely to pay back their loan are charged a higher rate of interest by banks. After each of the banks records its interest rates on the chalkboard, circle the rates and

the banks that will get the business. Explain to class that each depositor will naturally choose the bank that pays the highest interest rate, and each borrower will choose the bank that charges the lowest interest rate.

4. Assign Internet Economics for homework. This is a fun project that asks students to choose their dream house and then find out, using a bank's web site mortgage calculator, how much it really costs to buy that house—the monthly mortgage payment and the total amount (loan plus interest) that would be paid over 30 years. It's eye-opening! Have students share results and discuss.

Time Needed

1–2 class periods

Assessment and Evaluation

Assess accuracy of Personal Economics and Internet Economics homework. Do the answers and the numbers make sense?

Further Applications

If you were a bank loan officer, what specific questions would you ask of a customer, and what specific information would you require before you agreed to lend that person money? (What are you going to do with the money? How will you pay it back? May I see a salary stub, credit card bills, and tax return? Do you have other debts and expenses?)

 Web Sites

www.ubt.com
www.republicbank.com
www.eduloans.com

◆ SAVINGS AND BANKS, A KEY ECONOMIC INSTITUTION ◆

 ## *The Bottom Line*

Sometimes individuals and businesses don't have as much money as they'd like, so they borrow from a bank. But where does the bank get the money to lend? A few of the biggest banks get their money from the Federal Reserve, but all banks get money to lend from one very important source: savers.

Savers deposit their extra money, their savings, in banks in return for security and inter-est. But banks don't keep those deposits locked in the vault. Instead, they lend most of those deposits to individuals or businesses, charging them a higher rate of interest than the rate they pay their depositors. In this way, banks make a profit on the **spread**, or difference, between inter-est paid and interest charged. They act as the middleman between savers and borrowers. In this way, they help the economy grow by provid-ing money to individuals and businesses that need it and spend it.

 ## *Personal Economics*

This diagram illustrates a bank's middleman role in the economy. It also shows how banks make profits—accepting deposits and then lending them out.

Depositors put $ in bank for	Banks	Borrowers borrow $ from bank for
• Safekeeping • Check-writing privileges • Cash-dispensing privileges • Interest (Call a bank to find out what specific kinds of accounts pay interest): _____ _____ _____ _____ _____	• Safeguard $ • Clear checks • Dispense cash • Pay interest to depositors • Lend a significant portion of deposits to borrowers who need $ and, in the bank's judgment, are able to repay the loan plus interest by a certain date	• Loans that they promise to repay with interest by a set date (Call a bank to find out what specific kinds of loans you can get from the bank): _____ _____ _____ _____ _____ _____

(continued)

◆ SAVINGS AND BANKS, A KEY ECONOMIC INSTITUTION ◆ *(continued)*

📊 *Beyond the Bottom Line*

Note: Before you start this project, make sure you have read and understood Appendix II, "Finally, Understanding Interest and Interest Rates." You will be assigned jobs at one of six banks. All of these banks compete with each other for deposits and loans. Each bank will have several employees whose job is to figure out collectively what interest rate (in percent) different depositors should be paid and how much different borrowers should be charged.

The object of the project is to earn the highest possible profit for your bank without losing business to your competitors. Therefore, your discussion and your decisions should be kept confidential until the teacher calls on you. No spying. Assume projected **inflation** (a general increase in the price of all goods and services) of 3 percent for the coming year. This also means that a borrower must pay a lender more than 3 percent in interest for the lender to account for inflation *and* make a profit.

Each bank will be competing for the following customers:

- **Depositor 1** wants to deposit $10,000 in a savings account. Savings account holders are permitted only a few cash withdrawals a year. They must maintain a high average balance in their accounts. Determine what interest rate Depositor 1 should be paid by your bank: _____.
  Rationale: _____

- **Depositor 2** wants to deposit $10,000 in a checking account. Checking account holders are permitted unlimited cash withdrawals a year. They must maintain a minimal average balance in their accounts. Determine what interest rate Depositor 2 should be paid by your bank: _____.
  Rationale: _____

- **Depositor 3** wants to deposit $10,000 in a one-year certificate of deposit (CD). CD account holders are permitted no cash withdrawals whatsoever over the term of the CD (one year). Determine what interest rate Depositor 3 should be paid by your bank: _____.
  Rationale: _____

- **Borrower 1:** An established business wants to borrow $9,000 for one year for a capital purchase. Determine what interest rate Borrower 1 should be charged by your bank: _____.
  Rationale: _____

- **Borrower 2:** A 22-year-old individual wants to borrow $9,000 for one year to buy a used car. Determine what interest rate Borrower 2 should be charged by your bank: _____.
  Rationale: _____

- **Borrower 3:** A new business wants to borrow $9,000 to cover some salary expenses. Determine what interest rate Borrower 3 should be charged by your bank: _____.
  Rationale: _____

Each bank should then determine its overall dollar profit and its interest rate spread for the year, assuming an ability to do business with all three depositors and all three borrowers.

When the teacher gives the signal, representatives from each bank should approach the chalkboard at the same time, listing the interest rates their bank would pay and charge each of its customers. When all the interest rates have been listed on the chalkboard, the teacher will call on the employees from each bank to explain the interest rates they chose for each customer.

(continued)

 Activities for Economics Education

◆ SAVINGS AND BANKS, A KEY ECONOMIC INSTITUTION ◆ *(continued)*

Finally, the teacher will point out which depositors and which borrowers will do business with which banks. The teacher will help the class analyze the results.

 Internet Economics

An increasing number of banks have web sites describing the services they offer. The Union Bank & Trust Co. of Nebraska (**www.ubt.com**) and the Republic Bank & Trust Co. of Kentucky (**www.republicbank.com**) offer a wide variety of deposit and loan services to customers in their regions. Both banks offer competitive interest rates, which increase as savers deposit more and agree to withdraw less. They also offer various other features, like check-writing privileges and direct deposits.

For borrowers, Union and Republic offer an array of different loans. At Republic, you can even apply for a loan over the Internet, or by fax! Union boasts a separate web site with valuable information and links (**www.eduloans.com**) for students and parents preparing to pay for higher education. Union even has a mortgage calculator that will figure your monthly payment on a home mortgage loan. Simply input the amount of the loan (for example, $160,000), the interest rate (7 percent), and the number of years you will take to pay back the loan plus interest (30 years), and Union calculates your monthly mortgage payment ($1,064.49).

Find a house you like and try to figure out how much it would cost you to own it. Check newspaper ads for prices. Let's say your dream house is being sold for $250,000. The bank usually requires home buyers to put up at least 10 percent of the price in cash. This means the maximum you could borrow would be $225,000.

Check **www.interest.com** to determine current mortgage interest rates. Choose a fixed, not adjustable, interest rate, so you can see how much you're going to pay over the life of the mortgage. Choose how long you want to take to repay your mortgage. Terms are typically 15 or 30 years. For this exercise, choose a term of 30 years.

Now, find a bank web site that has a mortgage calculator (or use Union's), and input your numbers—amount of loan, interest rate, and term of loan. This will give your monthly mortgage payment! Finally, multiply this monthly payment by 360 (12 months times the 30 years of your loan equals 360 monthly payments). This will tell you how much it will really cost to buy your house.

Is it more than the amount you borrowed, the principal? Of course it is! Why? Interest, that's why. Lots and lots of interest adds up on a 30-year loan. Just think how much interest you would have saved if you could have paid for your house in cash. But few of us have the means to do that. So mortgages—and the banks that provide them—come in very handy, even if they are expensive.

Cost of house: _____

Amount borrowed: _____

Term of loan: _____

Interest rate: _____

Monthly payment: _____

Total cost (monthly payment × 360): _____

Cost of borrowing money (total cost – amount

    borrowed): _____

 Activities for Economics Education

ACTIVITY 13
MORE KEY PLAYERS AND KEY ECONOMIC INSTITUTIONS

Lesson Summary

Banks are not alone in playing an important role in our economy. Labor unions, entrepreneurs, and nonprofit organizations do also.

Objectives

- Students will understand what labor unions, entrepreneurs, and nonprofit organizations do and how they fit in our capitalist economy.

Directions

1. Have students read Labor Unions, starting with The Bottom Line. Discuss the role and image of unions. Ask students if they know anyone who belongs to a union.

2. Commence Beyond the Bottom Line. Divide the class into businesses (a total of nine students) and laborers (the remainder). Not every business will play every round, since there are specific numbers required: "Extras" should observe and/or help their team with comments and suggestions. Instruct laborers secretly that their **minimum hourly wage** rate—the rate below which they will not work—is $10/hour. Stress to businesses that they need to hire the required number of laborers or they will suffer financial losses. Follow directions carefully for the numbers of businesses and laborers required for each of the four rounds. Calculate the average wage negotiated for each of the four rounds. Prompt students to answer the questions posed. They should see the most important effect of labor unions on the negotiations—wages go up!

3. Assign Entrepreneurs, The Bottom Line, and Beyond the Bottom Line for homework. Students should be prepared to give a one-minute speech describing and "pitching" their entrepreneurial product in class the next day. List each of the products on the board and instruct students to vote with part or all of a hypothetical $100 for the products they liked best.

4. Then, have students read Nonprofit Organizations, The Bottom Line, and complete Personal Economics for homework.

5. Also assign Internet Economics for homework. It's very straightforward.

Time Needed

2–3 class periods

Assessment and Evaluation

The Beyond the Bottom Line homework will be assessed by other students during the sales pitches and the subsequent voting. The Personal Economics and Internet Economics homework is self-evident but should be checked for thoroughness and accuracy.

Further Applications

If our economy and society had to go without one of the key economic institutions/players described in this chapter, which should it be? Why?

 Web Sites

www.nwu.org
www.nabet.com
www.aflcio.org
www.sag.com
www.afm.org
www.mbemag.com

www.be-your-own-boss.com
www.marthastewart.com
www.scwca.org
www.cockatiels.org

◆ MORE KEY PLAYERS AND KEY ECONOMIC INSTITUTIONS ◆

Banks are not the only supporting player helping the individual and the business do business. Labor unions, entrepreneurs, and nonprofit organizations do not enjoy the economic clout or even the near-universal acceptance of banks. But there is little doubt that these three actors play important roles in our economy.

Labor Unions

 ### The Bottom Line

Labor unions represent about 15 percent of the U.S. labor force. They lobby for workers' jobs, rights, and compensation in negotiations with employers. Many union members work in blue-collar manufacturing industries, such as construction or mining. But unions also represent such diverse workers as public school teachers, Hollywood actors, and certain types of government employees.

 ### Beyond the Bottom Line

The class will be divided into businesses and laborers to play each of the four rounds described on the next page.

The objective of each business is to hire enough laborers to increase production and earn profits. In other words, if a business does not hire enough laborers to do the work needed, then it will suffer financial losses. At the same time, the business should try to limit the amount it spends on laborers' wages. Wages are a major cost that cuts into business profits.

The objective of all equally qualified laborers is to find work at a minimum wage of $___/hour (the teacher will give you this number—keep it secret from businesses), but preferably higher. The minimum wage is the amount a laborer needs to live; it is not the same as the official government-mandated "minimum wage." Assume that laborers have no incentive to work for less than their minimum demand of $___/hour.

Let the negotiations begin. One person should be in charge of each business. Businesses should try to hire a certain number of laborers at the lowest wage possible. Each laborer wants to find work at the highest wage possible. Each round lasts three minutes. At the end of each round, record the wages of each worker hired in dollars per hour. Calculate the average wage negotiated.

(continued)

◆ MORE KEY PLAYERS AND KEY ECONOMIC INSTITUTIONS ◆ *(continued)*

Business	Labor	Average Wage Negotiated
• Round 1: 4 businesses each need 5 workers	Pool of 25 workers	
• Round 2: 9 businesses each need 5 workers	Pool of 20 workers	
• Round 3: 4 businesses each need 5 workers	Pool of 25 workers, now represented by one union with sole responsibility for negotiating wages after consulting with the workers	
• Round 4: 9 businesses each need 5 workers	Pool of 20 workers, now represented by one union, as in Round 3	

Now answer these questions:

1. What has happened to the average wage for labor over the four rounds? _____

   _____

2. What effect did a shrinking labor pool (the supply of labor) have on the average wage from

   Round 1 to Round 2? From Round 3 to Round 4? _____

   _____

3. What effect did the number of businesses looking for laborers (the demand for labor) have on the

   average wage from Round 1 to Round 2? From Round 3 to Round 4? _____

   _____

4. Show on a graph using the supply and demand curves for labor the changes and results from
   Round 1 to Round 2. Place the average labor wage on the *y* axis and the quantity of labor on the
   x axis. Use the back of this sheet.

5. What effect did a labor union have on the average wage from Round 1 to Round 3? From

   Round 2 to Round 4? Why and how did it have this effect? _____

   _____

6. What happened to the extra workers in Rounds 1 and 3? In Round 3, how did the union decide

   to deal with this issue? _____

   _____

(continued)

◆ MORE KEY PLAYERS AND KEY ECONOMIC INSTITUTIONS ◆ *(continued)*

Entrepreneurs

The Bottom Line

Entrepreneurs are innovators and risk-takers. They are the people who create new markets for buyers and sellers, the ones who spur technological growth. They are the people who see opportunity in a desert. ("Let's design new irrigation techniques and sell them to farmers.") They see the possibilities in a computer network where information is scattered and hard to find. ("Let's invent a tool to search the Internet.") Entrepreneurs take risks organizing resources in the service of a new venture. But entrepreneurs can earn great rewards—profit, satisfaction, even recognition. There are also rewards for society—greater production, employment, competition, and tax dollars—if the entrepreneurial venture succeeds.

Beyond the Bottom Line

Here's your chance to become a successful entrepreneur! Think of a legitimate consumer need that's gone unfilled in today's marketplace. Now, try to come up with a good or service to address that need and make you a multimillionaire.

1. What's the perceived consumer need? _____

   _____

2. What's the specific good or service you want to offer these consumers? _____

   _____

3. How would you market this product to the public, your potential customers? Come up with an appropriate ad campaign to convince the public of your product's desirability.

   _____

You also need to sell your product. Prepare a brief (one-minute) persuasive speech. It should highlight the consumer need, describe the good/service, and praise the product's value.

As soon as all of the entrepreneurs have concluded their sales pitches, each student will receive $100. You must spend all, part, or none of that money on the products that have just been described and are now available, except for your own. The teacher will list each product on the board. Write next to the listed products how much of your $100 you would spend on each. For example, you may choose to spend $12 on Product 3, $77 on Product 8, $5 on Product 9, and $2 each on Products 14, 16, and 19.

My product choices: _____

_____

Which product earned the most consumer votes or dollars? _____

(continued)

Name_____ Date_____

◆ MORE KEY PLAYERS AND KEY ECONOMIC INSTITUTIONS ◆ *(continued)*

Nonprofit Organizations

💰 *The Bottom Line*

Nonprofit organizations make a variety of goods or services available to the general public. However, true to their name, they do not try to make a profit, as other businesses do. Any profits they do earn are not distributed to owners or investors. They are returned to the organization itself. Nonprofits are established for religious, health, educational, civic, or social purposes. They are exempt from certain taxes, since the government wants to promote the goods and services nonprofits provide to the public. Many nonprofits depend on financial assistance from their supporters.

🖩 *Personal Economics*

Make a list of the nonprofit organizations you have done business with. What goods/ services do they provide? If you're not sure whether an organization is a nonprofit and what they do, call them up and ask.

Nonprofit organization	Good/service provided to me
1.	
2.	
3.	

🖥 *Internet Economics*

Labor unions are well represented on the Web. The National Writers Union (**www.nwu.org/nwu/**) represents freelance writers. The National Association of Broadcast Employees and Technicians (NABET), at **www.nabet.com**, represents—you guessed it!—broadcast employees and technicians. NABET is directly affiliated with the AFL-CIO (**www.aflcio.org**). This is a huge federation with ties to most labor unions in the United States and Canada. Two of the more glamorous unions are the Screen Actors Guild, or SAG, at **www.sag.com**, and the American Federation of Musicians (AFM) at **www.afm.org**. After looking at their web sites, you'll see that unions are about more than maximizing salaries and benefits for members since some actors and rock stars earn millions of dollars every year!

There are various web sites offering resources for the budding entrepreneur. For example, there's the Minority Business Entrepreneur site (**www.mbemag.com**). This site promotes the mission of helping minorities and women in "creating and building wealth in all of our communities."

At the aptly named **www.be-your-own-boss.com**, information is offered about how to raise money from investors. To see an actual entrepreneur at work, and a famous and successful one at that, check out **www.marthastewart.com/nav/**. You'll discover you-know-who's many ventures.

(continued)

Activities for Economics Education

◆ MORE KEY PLAYERS AND KEY ECONOMIC INSTITUTIONS ◆ *(continued)*

Many nonprofit organizations advertise their causes on the Web and offer resources and information. The Southern California's Women's Caucus for Art web site (**www.scwca.org**) publicizes its commitment to the "cultural, aesthetic, and economic valuing of all women's art." Finally, there's the National Cockatiel Society (**www. cockatiels.org**). If you're not sure what a cockatiel is, check out this web site. And even if you do know, check it out anyway, because there's a lot more you could learn about cockatiels and their "keeping, breeding, and exhibiting."

Find one additional example of a union, an entrepreneur, and a nonprofit organization on-line. List addresses and give a brief summary of each.

Union

Name: _____

Web address: _____

_____

Summary: _____

_____

_____

Entrepreneur

Name: _____

Web address: _____

_____

Summary: _____

_____

_____

Nonprofit organization

Name: _____

Web address: _____

_____

Summary: _____

_____

_____

ACTIVITY 14

GOVERNMENT:
THE KEY ECONOMIC INSTITUTION

Lesson Summary

Apart from the individual and the business, the most important and influential economic player
in our capitalist economy is the government, which plays three vital roles:
(1) producer of goods and services; (2) tax collector; and (3) maker and enforcer of laws.

Objectives

- Students will see the extensive role and
  reach of the government into many areas
  of our lives: the goods and services we
  depend on, the taxes we pay, the conflicts
  we look to the government to settle.

Materials

- calculators
- copies of recent federal and state
  1040 forms

Directions

1. Have students read The Bottom Line.
   Discuss. Does our government do enough
   or does it try to do too much? What specific
   roles does the government perform well and
   which does it perform poorly?

2. Have students read Personal Economics—
   The Government as Producer of Goods and
   Services—and complete it, if able. If they
   can't think of some answers, instruct them
   to finish it for homework.

3. Beyond the Bottom Line, Figuring the First
   Family's Taxes is a fun and instructive in-
   class project or homework assignment, but
   you'll need to do some advance preparation. Specifically, you will need to make
   copies to hand out to students of the most
   recent federal (Form 1040) and corresponding state tax forms; you will also want to
   do this project yourself before you assign
   it to the students. In addition, make the
   appropriate adjustments in the student

instructions so that they fit with the latest
versions of the federal and state returns you
obtained. The numbers in "Figuring the First
Family's Taxes" are deliberately chosen
not to require students to fill out additional
forms beyond the 1040 and your state's
standard return. After students have filled
out the president's returns and answered
the questions, go over the returns in class,
using blank transparencies for the federal
and state tax forms and an overhead projec-
tor. Compare answers to questions. Note:
Define the term "tax bracket" for your
students and where to find it.

4. Have students read and complete Personal
   Economics—Property Rights and the Public
   Good. Compare student judges' decisions.
   Discuss.

5. Finally, assign Internet Economics for homework. Have students share their completed
   homework and discuss.

Time Needed

2–3 class periods

Assessment and Evaluation

Check the Personal Economics exercise
to see that students correctly identified government programs/products and explained how they
affect their lives. For Beyond the Bottom Line,
Figuring the First Family's Taxes, use the return
that you calculated beforehand as the "key,"
since tax returns vary from one state to another
and often from one year to the next. Evaluate the

(continued)

accuracy of Internet Economics homework: Are on-line congressional representatives correctly identified?

Further Applications

What constitutes a "fair" level of taxation? What changes, if any, in the current tax system would you propose to make the entire tax system fairer/better/more efficient?

 Web Sites

www.ed.gov
www.whitehouse.gov
www.irs.ustreas.gov
www.house.gov
www.senate.gov

www.fbi.gov
www.txdps.state.tx.us
www.ci.nyc.ny.us/
    html/nypd

◆ GOVERNMENT: *THE* KEY ECONOMIC INSTITUTION ◆

 ## *The Bottom Line*

Individuals and businesses hold the most prominent positions in our capitalist economy. Apart from them, the most important economic institution in our system is the government. The government includes federal, state, and local (county/city) government. It has tremendous influence on the actions of individuals and businesses, through its roles as:

1. the producer of goods and services that cannot or should not be produced by private companies;

2. the tax collector, who collects money from individuals and businesses to pay for government goods and services;

3. the maker and enforcer of laws to protect us and our property rights, and to safeguard the public good.

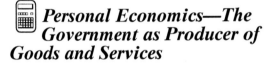 ## *Personal Economics—The Government as Producer of Goods and Services*

You may not have realized it, but the government makes, buys, or runs a lot of things. Like what? Check the phone book under the United States Government. Then make a list:

_____
_____
_____
_____
_____
_____
_____
_____

Which of these government programs affects you or your family?

_____
_____

 ## *Beyond the Bottom Line*

When the government spends money producing or buying goods and services, that money must come from somewhere. And that somewhere is your pocket. The government taxes individuals and businesses. Taxes are paid on income, profits, property, transactions, estates, and much more. This money pays for hundreds of billions of dollars of government programs every year. Does everybody pay taxes? Yes. Even the president? Of course!

(continued)

Name_____ Date_____

Figuring the First Family's Taxes

Instructions: You are the tax accountant for the president of the United States. The first family will be filing federal (Form 1040) and state tax returns for the current year. They've faxed you the following information:

D.C. residence:

1600 Pennsylvania Ave.
Washington, DC

One dependent daughter: Isabel

President's salary: $200,000 (actual presidential salary, unchanged since 1969)

Spouse's salary: $0

State residence:

(Pick a spot in your state.)

Refer to the federal return (Form 1040) with the following information:

- Taxable interest income (corporate bonds): $400
- Tax-exempt interest (municipal bonds): $200
- Dividend income (stocks): $250
- Capital gains (short-term): $10,000
- No IRA deductions
- Standard deduction (and exemptions—assume that they qualify)
- Use tax rate schedules to compute tax.
- President had $60,000 in federal taxes withheld from her pay.

Refer to the state return with the following information:

- Taxable income: Fill in Federal Adjusted Gross Income from Federal Form 1040, if applicable.
- No adjustments (subtractions or additions)
- Use tax rate schedule to compute tax.
- No credits or other taxes
- President had $10,000 in state taxes withheld from her pay.
- Contributions, if applicable—what would the president and her husband choose?

(continued)

◆ GOVERNMENT: *THE* KEY ECONOMIC INSTITUTION ◆ *(continued)*

Fill out the president's federal and state returns completely. Then, answer these questions:

1. What is the first family's total federal tax? Total state tax? Combined total tax? _____

    _____

2. Do they owe money or get a refund from the federal government? The state? _____

    _____

3. What is their federal tax bracket? State tax bracket? _____

    _____

4. What is their overall average tax rate? _____

5. Do you believe they pay too much in taxes? As their accountant, what would you propose the

    first family do to reduce their tax bite? _____

    _____

Personal Economics—Property Rights and the Public Good

Citizen (C): Property rights mean that my private property, my house, belongs to me. I have title to prove that I own it. One of the government's jobs is to protect and enforce any encroachments on my property. That is, after all, why we have laws prohibiting stealing, extortion, land fraud, and so forth. And we have a police force I can call to enforce them, and a court system designed to administer justice.

Government (G): Not so fast, bud. Didn't you forget something?

C: What?

G: The public good.

C: What does that have to do with my house?

G: Your house lies directly in the path of a planned highway. It will reduce traffic congestion on other streets in the neighborhood and boost economic growth in the downtown area. We, the government, need you to move now.

C: But that's my house!

G: We'll pay you for it.

C: But I don't want to sell!

G: See you in court.

    If you were the judge in a case like this, how would you decide this conflict between a private property right and the public good? Explain:

_____

_____

_____

◆ GOVERNMENT: *THE* KEY ECONOMIC INSTITUTION ◆ *(continued)*

Internet Economics

The government has many excellent web sites. They offer information about the countless services and goods available to the public, often at no charge. For example, the U.S. Department of Education (**www.ed.gov**) is one of many executive-branch departments with its own user-friendly site. It offers comprehensive educational statistics, help for students seeking financial aid, and information for students with disabilities.

You can also access other federal government web sites by first going to the White House web site at **www.whitehouse.gov**. You can say hello to the president. Then follow the link to "Commonly Requested Federal Services."

The role of the tax collector is played by the Internal Revenue Service, or IRS, a branch of the Department of Treasury. It is responsible for collecting taxes for the federal government. If you visit the IRS's web site, at **www.irs.ustreas.gov**, you might be surprised by how helpful those tax collectors are. The site offers help, extra tax forms, and many other services. It gives information on how to file your tax return electronically and, if you're lucky, get your refund deposited electronically to your bank account.

The government as lawmaker, enforcer, and justice provider is well documented on the Web.

The federal lawmaking, or legislative, branch is the Congress. You can learn all about both houses of Congress at **www.house. gov** and **www.senate.gov**.

Of course, laws mean little if they're not enforced. That's why we have agencies like the FBI at the federal level, the Texas Department of Public Safety at the state level, and the New York Police Department at the local level. Check out their interesting web sites at **www.fbi.gov/**, **www.txdps.state.tx.us/**, and **www.ci.nyc.ny.us/html/nypd/**, respectively.

Your representatives in Washington make laws that affect you. You have one congressman in the House of Representatives from your district and two senators from your state. Find out who represents you in Congress. E-mail one of them expressing your opinion about an issue that's important to your district or state or to the country as a whole. Make a copy of your e-mail and bring it to class.

Name of representative: _____

_____

E-mail address: _____

_____

GROSS DOMESTIC PRODUCT (GDP): EVERYTHING PLUS THE NEW KITCHEN SINK

Lesson Summary

Gross domestic product (GDP) is defined as the total market value of all new consumable and capital goods and services produced and sold in the economy in a given year. GDP is a key indicator, measured by the federal government, of national economic performance.

Objectives

- Students will be able to define, understand, and analyze GDP and its significance in the U.S. economy. In addition, students will learn the skills to designate expenditures on goods and services as specific components of the GDP formula, $C+I+G+(X–IM)$. They will then be able to ascertain, after comparing GDP totals over a certain period, whether the economy is healthy, prone to inflation, or in the throes of a recession or depression.

Materials

- calculators

Directions

1. Have students read The Bottom Line. Once students learn the definition of GDP, stress its significance as a key measure of national economic performance. For example, if "real" (inflation-adjusted) GDP increases by 3–4 percent annually, the economy is considered healthy; if real GDP increases by more than 4 percent, the economy is prone to inflation; if real GDP shows no increase or a prolonged decline, it is likely in a recession or depression.

2. Have students read and complete Personal Economics and share answers with the class.

3. Next, assign Beyond the Bottom Line for in-class work or homework. Tell students they must know and apply (1) the precise definition of GDP ("the total market value of all *new consumable* and *capital* goods and services *produced and sold* in the economy *in a given year*"); (2) the equation

$(C+I+G+(X–IM))$; and (3) the significance of a rise or fall or no movement in GDP (as summarized above).

4. Assign Internet Economics for homework. Have students share their completed homework and discuss.

Time Needed

1–2 class periods

Assessment and Evaluation

For Personal Economics, check to see that students accurately complete the lists of goods and services that people might buy fewer of in a recession, when they have less money to spend. The Bottom Line GDP calculations in Beyond the Bottom Line are $111,170,000 for 2006 and $111,510,000 for 2007. The 2007 economy was probably in a recession, since GDP rose by a minuscule 0.3 percent in the past year. For Internet Economics, the questions call for factual answers after a comparison of your Federal Reserve District's economic health with the U.S. economy as a whole.

Further Applications

What specific line-item expenditures featured in Beyond the Bottom Line suggest that GDP may *not* necessarily be an accurate measure of the nation's economic well-being? (The clean-up and repair costs in Santa Monica Bay and Johnstown.)

 Web Sites

www.rich.frb.org
www.federalreserve.gov

◆ GROSS DOMESTIC PRODUCT (GDP): EVERYTHING PLUS THE NEW KITCHEN SINK ◆

The Bottom Line

The government plays a key economic role, as described in the last activity. It also plays a fundamental part in measuring, analyzing, and directing the entire U.S. economic system. One of the key economic measures that the government oversees is **gross domestic product**, or GDP.

GDP is the basic measure of a nation's annual economic output and income. It is the total market value, measured in dollars, of all new consumable and capital goods and services produced and sold in the economy in a given year. GDP is important. If it were flat or fell slightly, it would suggest an economy in trouble. Reduced output means lower profits for businesses, and less income for owners. As a result, some workers could lose their jobs. This, in turn, would result in higher unemployment.

On the other hand, an increased GDP suggests a healthy economy. If the nation's economic output rose by a healthy amount, say 4 percent, the economy would likely be in much better shape. Increased output means bigger profits, higher income, and jobs for almost everyone—lower unemployment.

Ironically, GDP can rise too much, say 5 percent or more. Then most economists would say that the economy is in trouble. Why? If an economy is producing too much, too fast, then **inflation**, a general rise in prices, could be triggered. Inflation is also a key economic indicator.

Whatever the economic scenario, GDP can tell us a lot about the relative health of a nation's economy. This makes it easier for the government and the people to prepare for the consequences of changes in the economy.

Personal Economics

"You know, I don't really care one bit about GDP. It must be a big pain for the government to measure, and it doesn't affect me or my business in the slightest." Oh, really?

First of all, it's not difficult for the government to calculate GDP, though it is a huge number—about $9 trillion! The government simply adds:

1. the amount consumers pay for any new goods and services, called **consumption** (C), to

2. the amount that businesses spend on new capital goods and individuals pay for new houses, called **investment** (I), to

3. the amount that the government spends on new goods and services, called **government spending** (G), to

4. the amount that foreigners pay for new exports (X) (domestic goods and services sold abroad) minus the amount that Americans pay for new imports (IM) (foreign goods and services purchased here), called **net exports** (X–IM). (The dollars spent on foreign imports is considered a negative in U.S. GDP calculations. When someone buys a foreign import, those dollars ultimately leave the U.S. and end up abroad.)

This annual total is called **nominal GDP**. So, the applicable formula is C+I+G+(X–IM)=nominal GDP.

Secondly, GDP <u>is</u> important to you and your business. If the economy slows down—a condition called a **recession**—consumers may have less income to spend on goods and services. And **depression**—a long, deep recession characterized by falling GDP and huge unemployment—is even worse. Make a list of goods and services that might be adversely affected by a recession.

Automobiles, vacations, _____

_____

_____ (continued)

Activities for Economics Education

◆ GROSS DOMESTIC PRODUCT (GDP):
EVERYTHING PLUS THE NEW KITCHEN SINK ◆ *(continued)*

On a personal level, what goods and services would you cut out if you suddenly had less income?

_____

_____

_____

An economy that speeds up too much and triggers inflation can also affect you and your business. Why? An inflationary rise in prices is clearly bad news for you, the consumer. But it can also be harmful for you, the business person, since inflation boosts the prices of inputs, which raises your production costs.

Hence, either inflation or the opposite, a recession or depression, will affect you and your business. So you had best be prepared. The government's measure of GDP helps.

Beyond the Bottom Line

Here is a list of imaginary items. If they were real, which of them would be counted in 2007 calculations of GDP? Which would be counted in 2006 calculations of GDP? Which would not be counted in either year?

Now, designate the items as belonging to one of the five component groups: consumption (*C*), investment (*I*), government spending (*G*), exports (*X*), or imports (*IM*). Write the designation and the dollar amount in the appropriate column in the chart on page 62. Sum up GDP totals for both years. Then determine the state of the 2007 economy if GDP were based solely on these imaginary items.

1. '06 Ford bought new in '06 for $15,000 and resold as a used car in '07 for $12,000.

2. Government spent $100 million on one B-1 bomber in '06 and $63 million on some smaller planes in '07.

3. Legal services billed and paid in '06: $5,000.

4. Legal services billed and paid in '07: $10,000.

5. Brand-new house bought in '06: $150,000.

6. Previously owned house bought in '07: $175,000.

7. Chrysler paid $30 million for a new plant in '06 and $8 million for new machinery in '07.

8. U.S. imported $100 million worth of autos in '06 and exported $80 million worth of computers in '06.

9. U.S. imported $80 million worth of autos in '07 and exported $100 million worth of computers in '07.

10. Bay Jet-Skis produced and sold jet-skis worth $1 million in '06; state of California spent $500,000 in '07 to clean up waste in Santa Monica Bay caused by Bay Jet-Ski plant.

11. Federal, state, and local governments spent $20 million to repair damage from the '07 Johnstown flood.

(continued)

         Activities for Economics Education

Name_____ Date _____

◆ GROSS DOMESTIC PRODUCT (GDP):
EVERYTHING PLUS THE NEW KITCHEN SINK ◆ (continued)

Item	2006 GDP Designation	$ Amount	2007 GDP Designation	$ Amount
1.				
2.				
3.				
4.				
5.				
6.				
7.				
8.				
9.				
10.				
11.				
	Totals: 2006 GDP _____		Totals: 2007 GDP _____	

What is the state of the 2007 economy: recession, depression, or inflationary?

_____

Explain: _____

_____

_____

How much would the GDP have to rise or fall in 2007 before the U.S. economy could be called healthy?

In other words, calculate a new and improved 2007 GDP number _____.

(continued)

◆ GROSS DOMESTIC PRODUCT (GDP): EVERYTHING PLUS THE NEW KITCHEN SINK ◆ *(continued)*

Internet Economics

Several web sites offer interesting information about the nation's economic output, or GDP. The Federal Reserve Bank in Richmond, Virginia, offers an excellent site (**www.rich.frb.org**). It contains key information about the regional economic output of the Fifth Federal Reserve District. The fifth district covers the economies of Virginia, Maryland, North Carolina, South Carolina, Washington, D.C., and most of West Virginia. It accounts for nearly 10 percent of total U.S. GDP.

For those of you interested in your own region's and the country's economic performance, check out **www.federalreserve.gov**. This is the home page for the Federal Reserve Bank. Follow the links to the Beige Book, found under "Monetary Policy." The "Book" contains extensive data and analysis on all 12 Federal Reserve districts and on the U.S. economy as a whole.

Find your own Federal Reserve district. What states does it include? What is the current economic health of your district/region? How does your district's economy compare to the nation's as a whole? In what ways is your district's economy stronger than the nation's? In what ways is it weaker? As you fill in your answers below, cite specific data wherever possible.

State: _____

Federal Reserve district: _____

States included in district: _____

_____

_____

Current economic health of your district: _____

_____

_____

Area in which your district's economy is stronger than nation's: _____

_____

_____

Areas in which your district's economy is weaker than nation's: _____

_____

_____

ACTIVITY 16

INFLATION: THE DOLLAR'S BIGGEST ENEMY HAS A FEW FRIENDS

Lesson Summary

Inflation is more than a general increase in prices for goods and services. Inflation reduces the value of everyone's money, which makes it vastly unpopular. However, when it is unexpected, inflation has its share of beneficiaries, too.

Objectives

- Students will understand the effects of inflation by experiencing for themselves the dollar-sapping power of inflation. They will also observe both the positive and negative impacts of unexpected inflation, and understand what people do when they anticipate inflation.

Directions

1. Have students read The Bottom Line. Ask them if they have seen evidence of rising prices in the last year.

2. Immediately commence Personal Economics. Students should be able to grasp quickly the significant impact of inflation on the value—the purchasing power—of money.

3. Next, assign Beyond the Bottom Line for in-class work or homework. Make sure students understand the basic premise: Unexpected inflation harms people who have **lent money at a fixed interest rate** or agreed to receive money in the future (in a contract, for example), assuming that prices would go up only so much. Unexpected inflation helps people who have **borrowed money at a fixed interest rate** or agreed to pay money in the future. Naturally, if potential losers or victims correctly anticipate inflation, they can make the proper adjustments: raise interest rates on loans or demand more money in their contract.

4. Assign Internet Economics for homework. Most of the work required involves simple reporting, but the last series of questions asks students where they would most like to live. Students must then find out, using a cost-of-living calcula-

tor, how much more or less it would cost them, because of inflation, to live in that city compared to their hometown.

Time Needed

1–2 class periods

Extensions

If you wish, distribute Appendix III, Calculating Inflation: Your Own Personal Consumer Price Index (CPI).

Assessment and Evaluation

Beyond the Bottom Line answers follow: Unexpected inflation helps the renter, the employer, the U.S. government, the borrower, and you. If inflation had been correctly anticipated, the U.S. citizen, the bank, and I would have demanded a higher rate of interest as compensation for inflation and our loss of purchasing power. Likewise, the landlord and the worker would have demanded more money in the future for the same reason. The data found by students to answer the Internet Economics questions could be the basis of an interesting class discussion.

Further Applications

What makes inflation easier to deal with? (Rising salaries, which tend to move up as inflation rises because workers don't want to see their purchasing power erode!)

 Web Sites

stats.bls.gov/cpihome.htm
www.westegg.com/inflation
www.homefair.com/homefair/cmr/salcalc.html

◆ INFLATION: THE DOLLAR'S BIGGEST ENEMY HAS A FEW FRIENDS ◆

 ## The Bottom Line

Inflation is more than just an increase in the general price level of goods and services. Inflation reduces the value of everyone's money. That makes inflation extremely unpopular. But you know what? Although inflation has its enemies and victims, it also has a few friends and beneficiaries.

Personal Economics

You have $20 in your wallet. What can you buy with that money? Go ahead; make a list.

Item:	Price:
Total:	$20 (approximate)

Now, assume inflation strikes. Every item you listed doubles in price, a 100 percent increase! Now make a new list. Include only the items you listed before that you can still buy with your $20.

Item:	Price:
Total:	$20 (approximate)

Your $20 is worth a lot less now because it buys fewer items. In fact, it's worth 50 percent less than its preinflation value. You simply cannot buy all of the things you bought before with your money because your money is worth less. Not worthless—not yet, anyway—but worth less.

(continued)

◆ INFLATION: THE DOLLAR'S BIGGEST ENEMY
HAS A FEW FRIENDS ◆ *(continued)*

◈ *Beyond the Bottom Line*

So inflation has its victims—everyone with a dollar in her pocket. On the other hand, inflation has some beneficiaries, too. For example, if you borrowed money at a fixed interest rate before a higher rate of inflation was even anticipated, you're a beneficiary, a winner! Why? Because you're now paying back your loan at a below-market interest rate with dollars worth less than your lender originally anticipated. You've made out at the expense of the person who lent you money. In general, when a higher rate of inflation strikes unexpectedly, **creditors**—people who have lent money—lose. **Debtors**—people who have borrowed and still owe money—win. Wealth, in the form of increased purchasing power, is actually redistributed from creditors to debtors. Of course, when inflation subsides unexpectedly, debtors lose and creditors win. Then wealth is redistributed from debtors to creditors.

Inflation's Victims and Beneficiaries

Assume inflation has unexpectedly jumped from 3 percent, an almost constant level for many years, to 10 percent this year. Take the following pairs. Split them up according to who suffers and who gains during this period of climbing inflation. Be prepared to explain your choices.

Parties	Relationship
1. Renter/Landlord	➜ Signed one-year lease just before inflation jumped
2. Worker/Employer	➜ Signed three-year contract last year
3. U.S. Government/ U.S. Citizen	➜ Citizen bought a five-year U.S. Treasury Bond two years ago. (Note: A bond is a written promise to repay a loan.)
4. Bank/Borrower	➜ Home owner has 30-year mortgage on property bought last year.
5. You/Me	➜ You borrowed $1,000 from me at 6 percent interest.

Higher Inflation's Victim   **Higher Inflation's Beneficiary**

1. _____   _____

Explanation: _____

_____

2. _____   _____

Explanation: _____

_____

(continued) ◉

◆ INFLATION: THE DOLLAR'S BIGGEST ENEMY
HAS A FEW FRIENDS ◆ *(continued)*

Higher Inflation's Victim   **Higher Inflation's Beneficiary**

3. _____   _____

   Explanation: _____

   _____

4. _____   _____

   Explanation: _____

   _____

5. _____   _____

   Explanation: _____

   _____

OK, let's change a key assumption. The approaching higher inflation is still a reality. But now it has been fully expected and correctly anticipated by all of the people above. Explain what adjustments these individuals, businesses, and the government would make in their relationships to prepare for this surging inflation. Are there still victims and beneficiaries?

1. Adjustments: _____

   _____

2. Adjustments: _____

   _____

3. Adjustments: _____

   _____

4. Adjustments: _____

   _____

5. Adjustments: _____

   _____

(continued)

◆ INFLATION: THE DOLLAR'S BIGGEST ENEMY
HAS A FEW FRIENDS ◆ *(continued)*

Internet Economics

There's some great stuff on the Internet about inflation, including some hands-on sites that allow you to see firsthand the devastating effect inflation has on the value of a dollar.

But first, visit the Bureau of Labor Statistics' inflation link at **stats.bls.gov/cpihome.htm**. The BLS is an agency in the U.S. Department of Labor. It is responsible for collecting, analyzing, and distributing official inflation data, updated every month. Read the **Consumer Price Index** (CPI) summary. This shows the changes in price levels for a variety of goods and services in metropolitan areas around the country.

Now go beyond the mere reporting of CPI results. Which types of goods and services rose the most in price in the last month, or the last year? Which goods and services rose the least, or dropped in price, in the last month, or the last year? Which cities had the highest overall price levels? Which had the lowest overall price levels? Did the answers surprise you? Or did they confirm what you thought about the nation's most inflationary—and deflationary—goods, and most and least expensive places to live?

There's a great inflation application, a cost-of-living analysis, at **www.homefair.com/ homefair/cmr/salcalc.html**. Some cities are more expensive to live in than others; they experience higher inflation. Have you ever wondered by how much? Now you can enter your home state, town or city, and your current salary. (Make it up if you're not working.) Enter the city and state where you'd like to live. The cost-of-living analysis will calculate the salary you would need in your new town to match the buying power of your salary in your old hometown. By how much should your salary change to maintain your purchasing power if you moved to, say, New York City? Little Rock, Arkansas? Fairbanks, Alaska?

Current city: _____

Current salary: _____

New city: _____

Salary needed to maintain purchasing power:

_____

Percent salary change: _____

At **www.westegg.com/inflation**, you can experience for yourself the dollar-eroding power of inflation. The site boasts an "inflation calculator." It will "adjust any given amount of money for inflation." For example, if you received $100 from your grandparents the year you were born, what would a gift of equivalent purchasing power be today? I won't tell you when I was born, but I will tell you that it would take $560.05 in 1999 to buy what $100 bought in the year of my birth. That's a lot of inflation, and I'm not that old. Really.

Check and see what $100 in the year of your birth would be worth today as a result of inflation.

Birth year: _____

Value of $100 today: _____

ACTIVITY 17

UNEMPLOYMENT:
WHO'S WORKING AND WHO ISN'T

Lesson Summary

Unemployment is defined as those people in the civilian labor force, 16 years and older, who are willing and able to work and actively looking for a job, but are unable to get one. There are three broad categories of unemployment: frictional unemployment, structural unemployment, and cyclical unemployment. The personal and societal costs of unemployment can be considerable.

Objectives

- Students will be able to define and understand unemployment and its consequences and distinguish among its various types. They will also see for themselves the significant costs of unemployment for a family, a community, a society.

Directions

1. Have students read The Bottom Line.

2. Immediately commence Personal Economics. After students make their determinations as to who counts as unemployed, discuss. Some people without work who are able to work are not counted as officially unemployed. Should they be?

3. Next assign Beyond the Bottom Line for in-class work or homework. Encourage students to think about the monetary and nonmonetary costs of unemployment from different perspectives (personal, business, societal).

4. Assign Internet Economics for homework. Most of the questions involve simple research, though the last one encourages reasoned speculation and some knowledge of the local unemployment picture.

Time Needed

1–2 class periods

Assessment and Evaluation

Answers to questions in Personal Economics are Joey (NLF), Uncle Paul (U-F), Aunt Millie (U-C), Mario (NLF), Jan (NLF), Hiroko (U-S). Check to see that students' answers in Beyond the Bottom Line are reasoned and reasonable. Check for the same in Internet Economics answers. You should also check for accuracy by accessing the official unemployment numbers at the U.S. Labor Department's Bureau of Labor Statistics' web site.

Extensions

If you wish, distribute Appendix IV, Calculating Unemployment: Your Own Local Unemployment Rate.

Further Applications

Why do you think that there are significant differences in unemployment rates between young and old, men and women, different races, and high school dropouts and college grads? (A comprehensive question deserves a comprehensive answer. Here's a start anyway: experience, education, skills, alternatives to labor, discrimination, ability to train, and so forth.)

 **Web Sites**

stats.bls.gov

◆ UNEMPLOYMENT: WHO'S WORKING AND WHO ISN'T ◆

 ## The Bottom Line

Unemployment exists officially when people in the civilian labor force, 16 years and older, are willing and able to work and actively looking for a job, but can't find one. The **unemployment rate** is the number of people unemployed divided by the number of people in the civilian labor force. It is expressed as a percentage.

There are various categories of the unemployed. They include: workers between jobs (frictional unemployment); workers whose industries and skills have been rendered obsolete by a changing economy (structural unemployment); and workers whose jobs have been lost because of general economic factors, like a recession (cyclical unemployment). Still, the key conditions in determining whether someone is officially unemployed are "no job, but ready and looking."

While some unemployment is unavoidable, its costs can be considerable to individuals and their families, as well as to society as a whole.

 ## Personal Economics

Here is a list of friends and relatives. Label them as either employed (E), unemployed (U), or not in the labor force (NLF). For the unfortunate friends who are unemployed (U), further characterize their unemployment as frictional (U-F), structural (U-S), or cyclical (U-C).

- Joey, age 15; dropped out of high school; can't find a job._____

- Uncle Paul, age 32; left Riley Auto Sales to find a new job across town._____

- Aunt Millie, age 38; laid off at the beginning of a recession; desperate for work._____

- Mario, age 50; quit his job after winning the lottery; enjoying early retirement. _____

- Jan, age 23; fired from last job, but not looking for work right now._____

- Hiroko, age 58; formerly a top engineer in the nearly obsolete LP record industry until her employer went out of business; looking to find a position in the CD industry._____

 ## Beyond the Bottom Line

Jim is married and a father of three. He recently lost his job when his company went out of business. He qualified for some temporary unemployment compensation from the state and his family had some limited savings. Still, these monies only partly covered the loss of his income. Assume that Jim is your dad. What is the cost of his unemployment, in monetary and nonmonetary terms, to your family?

_____

_____

_____

_____

What specific goods and services would your family have to do without if your family's income dropped by 50 percent? How would your behavior change?

_____

_____

_____

_____

(continued)

◆ UNEMPLOYMENT: WHO'S WORKING AND WHO ISN'T ◆ *(continued)*

What is the cost of Jim's unemployment, in monetary and nonmonetary terms, to society?

_____

_____

_____

_____

What specific businesses might be affected by your family's loss of income?

_____

_____

_____

_____

Summarize the overall monetary and non-monetary costs of unemployment.

_____

_____

_____

_____

_____

🖥️ *Internet Economics*

The U.S. Labor Department's Bureau of Labor Statistics (**stats.bls.gov**) is the place to find unemployment data. Check out the "Economy at a Glance" section to see what the latest unemployment picture looks like. For an excellent explanation of the methods used to calculate unemployment, follow the links to "How the Government measures unemployment" (under "Publications and Other Documentation"). For even more specific data, follow the links to the

news releases and regional sections (under "Related Programs"). At the news releases site, study the unemployment data. They are organized by age, gender, race, and educational attainment.

Using the BLS site for reference, answer the following questions:

What is the current national unemployment rate?

_____

What has been the trend in unemployment over the last 12 months?

_____

_____

Which groups have the highest and lowest rates of unemployment?

_____

_____

How do teenagers fare? _____

_____

At the regional site, find out how your region/metropolitan area is doing.

Is the local unemployment rate higher or lower than the national rate?

_____

Why do you think that there is or might be a difference?

_____

_____

_____

ACTIVITY 18

FISCAL AND MONETARY POLICY: DIRECTING THE ECONOMY TO AN IDEAL LEVEL

Lesson Summary

The U.S. economy is strongly influenced by **fiscal policy**, the determination of spending and tax levels by Congress and the president, and **monetary policy**, the determination of the money supply and certain interest rates by the Federal Reserve.

Objectives

- Students will see how and why fiscal policy (FP) and monetary policy (MP) can work to improve the nation's economy, slowing it down when it's growing too fast (suggesting high inflation) or speeding it up when it's growing too slowly or even declining (suggesting a recession or depression). Students will also understand that FP is subject to intense debate, negotiation, and compromise within Congress and between Congress and the president, while MP is formulated by one body, the Board of Governors of the Federal Reserve.

Directions

1. Have students read The Bottom Line. Make sure they understand these policies and their intended objective: moving the economy toward a state characterized by healthy GDP growth (about 3–4 percent annually), low inflation (2–3 percent), and low unemployment (4–5 percent).

2. Commence Beyond the Bottom Line. Divide the class into three groups and follow the directions carefully. The project has three stages and will likely last the entire class period. If there's time, lead the class in an analysis of the project—and FP/MP—after the third round by asking the questions posed. If not, assign the questions for homework, which students can do alone or in pairs, and then go over the answers and opinions in class the next time.

3. If students can download material from the Web, also assign Internet Economics for homework: It's an FP/MP game, and it's fun!

Time Needed

2 class periods

Assessment and Evaluation

The first three Beyond the Bottom Line questions are based on the specific policies developed and processes followed by the in-class groups (president, Congress, and the Federal Reserve). Check to see that students correctly understand MP and FP and their consequences. You may want to talk about MP and FP effects on interest rates if the other consequences are clear. For the Internet Economics homework, you might want to ask students for a printout of the results, if possible, to confirm that they did in fact play the San Francisco Fed's interactive FP/MP game.

Further Applications

Ask students to develop the appropriate MP and FP to deal with the following more advanced and more difficult economic situation: Real GDP growth rate— 0.0 percent; unemployment—8.0 percent; inflation— 10.0 percent. Students should choose an FP and an MP that will try to correct this economic "stagflation." There are no easy solutions to "stagflation," but it's fun and instructive to try to identify one.

 Web Sites

www.federalreserve.gov
woodrow.mpls.frb.fed.us
www.ny.frb.org
www.whitehouse.gov/omb
www.frbsf.org

www.cbo.gov
www.frbsf.org/
econedu/
curriculum/
monetary.hqx

◆ FISCAL AND MONETARY POLICY: DIRECTING THE ECONOMY TO AN IDEAL LEVEL ◆

💰 *The Bottom Line*

The U.S. economy is measured by key indicators: output (GDP), prices (inflation), and unemployment. It can be directed, with some success, through the following:

1. **Fiscal policy** (FP) decisions, made by the president and Congress. These change spending and tax levels. If the economy is slow, the president and Congress may decide on an **expansionary** fiscal policy. This means increasing government spending and cutting taxes. These changes should boost output, employment, and prices. If the economy is moving too fast, the president and Congress may choose a **contractionary** FP. This calls for cutting government spending and increasing taxes. These changes should slow or lower output, employment, and prices.

2. **Monetary policy** (MP) decisions, made by the Federal Reserve (Fed). These change the supply of money in the economy and the availability of loans, which are sensitive to interest rates. If the economy is slow, the Fed may decide on an **expansionary** MP. This is a policy to expand the money supply. This can be done by buying government bonds and lowering the discount rate and the bank reserve requirement. These changes will lower interest rates and boost output, employment, and prices. If the economy is moving too fast, the Fed may choose a **contractionary** MP. This is a policy to contract the money supply. This can be done by selling government bonds and raising the discount rate and the bank reserve requirement. These changes will increase interest rates and slow or lower output, employment, and prices.

Here's a quick review of how fiscal and monetary policies work. An expansionary policy is one that "expands" the economy. The government and the Fed have the tools to swell the amount of money in the economy. That expands income, spending, and production. A contractionary policy is one that contracts or shrinks the economy. The government and the Fed have the tools to reduce the amount of money in the economy. That shrinks income, spending, and production.

Fiscal Policy	
Expansionary:	Cut taxes Increase government spending
Contractionary:	Increase taxes Cut government spending
Monetary Policy	
Expansionary:	Increase money supply by buying government bonds Decrease interest rates
Contractionary:	Decrease money supply by selling government bonds Increase interest rates

The ultimate goal is to move the economy to a perfect state, or to keep it there! This economic state is characterized by healthy GDP growth (about 4 percent), low inflation (2–3 percent), and low unemployment (4–5 percent).

(continued)

◆ FISCAL AND MONETARY POLICY:
DIRECTING THE ECONOMY TO AN IDEAL LEVEL ◆ *(continued)*

Beyond the Bottom Line

The class will be divided into three groups: the presidency, Congress, and the Federal Reserve. The presidency and Congress will first work separately and then together on FP. The Fed will work on MP. The FP and MP people may talk to each other, but they must work and make policy separately. All three groups are responsible for directing and managing the U.S. economy. Here's the situation:

Real GDP growth rate: 5.0 percent

Unemployment: 2.5 percent

Inflation: 12.0 percent

The president, Congress, and the Fed have their work cut out for them. The economy is moving much too fast. GDP growth and inflation are above ideal levels. Unemployment is below target rates. What should be done to FP and MP?

First, the three groups will meet separately for 10 minutes to:

A. Identify the specific problems and the costs to society of not taking action;

B. Suggest specific policies to combat the problems;

C. Predict the short- and long-term effects, positive and negative, of their policies.

Each group should file a written report, detailing their responses/approaches to A, B, and C. The report should be based on majority votes within the group. Each group should appoint a leader responsible for keeping the meeting on track and on schedule.

Second, the president and Congress will meet together for 10 minutes to discuss their FP recommendations. For FP recommendations to

become law, Congress must pass them with a majority vote. The president must sign them, also with majority approval of the presidency group. Thus, the two groups need to file a joint President-Congress FP report detailing the approved FP measures.

During this time, the Fed continues to meet as before. If the majority of the Fed group expresses approval for an MP action, that action takes effect at a time that should be noted. Approved MP policies should be noted on the Fed group's written report.

Third, bring the fiscal and monetary policy groups together. Have representatives summarize on the chalkboard, and then in a short speech, the policies approved by majorities in each group. The representatives should also summarize the predicted effects of these policies on GDP growth, unemployment, inflation, and interest rates.

Your teacher will then ask your class a series of questions:

1. Do you believe that your group's fiscal or monetary policies will improve the current economic situation? In what areas? Where and how might your policies fall short?

2. Do you believe that the other groups' fiscal or monetary policies will improve the current economic situation? In what areas? Where and how might their policies fall short?

3. Which group had the advantage of being able to pass and implement policy more quickly? Why? Which group had the advantage of being able to pass and implement policy that will likely affect more people in the long run? Why?

(continued)

◆ Fiscal and Monetary Policy: Directing the Economy to an Ideal Level ◆ *(continued)*

Internet Economics

Web sites offering a close-up, firsthand view of monetary and fiscal policy are plentiful on the Net.

Naturally, the best place to find information about monetary policy is to go straight to the source: the Federal Reserve. You can visit the Fed's home site, produced by its Board of Governors, at **www.federalreserve.gov**. It offers a wealth of useful information and statistics.

I prefer some of the regional Fed sites: the Minneapolis Fed (**woodrow.mpls.frb.fed.us**), which contains an excellent explanation of the Fed's open market operations ("What is the FOMC?"); the New York Fed (**www.ny.frb.org**), which offers a hands-on FOMC simulation project (under "Economic Education"); and the San Francisco site (**www.frbsf.org**), which concisely summarizes monetary policy.

You can also go straight to the sources for information about fiscal policy. At the White House, the group in charge of the federal budget is the Office of Management and Budget (**www.whitehouse.gov/omb**). The OMB's job is "to assist the President in overseeing the preparation of the Federal budget and to supervise its administration in the Executive Branch agencies." At its web site, the OMB offers all kinds of information about the budget. It also shows the major steps that must be taken for the budget to become official. One of those steps is giving Congress an opportunity to respond to the president's proposed budget and come up with one of their own for the president's signature or veto.

The Congressional Budget Office (**www.cbo.gov**), Congress's equivalent of the OMB, provides Congress "with objective, timely, nonpartisan analyses needed for economic and budget decisions . . . and information and estimates required for the Congressional budget process." The annual federal budget involves decisions about government spending and taxing. This is the essence of fiscal policy. Its passage, which requires the consent of Congress and the president, is a huge undertaking.

Explore the San Francisco Fed web site again. Find the two excellent interactive computer simulations of fiscal and monetary policy. Try to download them, with your teacher's permission. You play the president in one simulation and the Chairman of the Fed in the other. As you make fiscal or monetary policy decisions, the effects of your actions are revealed in inflation and unemployment data and ultimately in the overall verdict: You've been elected/defeated in your re-election bid; or you've been reappointed/fired as Chairman of the Fed! These fiscal and monetary policy simulations are fun, informative, and challenging! You'll find them at **www.frbsf. org/econedu/curriculum/monetary.hqx**.

INTERNATIONAL CURRENCY EXCHANGE: DOLLARS AND SENSE

Lesson Summary

An exchange rate is the price of one nation's currency in terms of another's, and like other prices, it is determined by the forces of supply and demand. A strong local currency means lower prices for imported goods; a weak local currency means that exported goods are more affordable abroad.

Objectives

- Students will learn how to convert money from one currency to another and will experience for themselves the effect of a declining or increasing currency exchange rate on their purchasing power.

Materials

- daily newspaper with a currency exchange table
- calculators

Directions

1. Have students read The Bottom Line. Stress the fact that currency fluctuations can be explained simply on one graph by demand and supply curves for one currency only; however, the equilibrium price of that one currency is expressed in terms of the other currency.

2. Commence Personal Economics; students should be able to finish these problems in class with time left for clarifications and corrections, if necessary. Make sure you have a daily paper with currency exchange rates available for students.

3. Start Beyond the Bottom Line. Students will need to finish this project for homework.

4. Also assign Internet Economics for homework. The questions involve facts, which can be gathered at the web sites listed, and opinion. Any knowledge you have of the

European Union (Europe's NAFTA, if you will) will be valuable.

Time Needed

2 class periods

Assessment and Evaluation

Answers to Personal Economics questions follow:

- $100=6,500/7,000 Spanish pesetas
- 1 Spanish peseta=$0.015/$0.014.
- 1,000 Spanish pesetas=$15.38/$14.29.

Answers to Beyond the Bottom Line questions follow:

1. $753
2. 132,750 yen
3. $0.00667
4. $666.67
5. 150,000 yen
6. The price of Japanese stereos in the U.S. declines; the price of U.S. computers in Japan increases.
7. U.S. imports and Japanese exports increase; Japanese imports and U.S. exports decrease.
8a. Exports will decline and imports will increase because the new prices will affect quantity demanded in both countries.

8b. Exports will increase and imports will decline because the new prices will affect quantity demanded in both countries.

Special Bonus Question: Lovers of a strong U.S. dollar (the rest are haters)—foreign producers of American imports, American consumers, American tourists traveling abroad.

Check the accuracy of the Internet Economics assignment by linking to the web sites listed.

Further Applications

Have students practice drawing and analyzing supply and demand curves as they shift for a specific currency and discussing the consequences.

 Web Sites

www.xe.net/ucc
www.europa.eu.int.

◆ INTERNATIONAL CURRENCY EXCHANGE: DOLLARS AND SENSE ◆

The Bottom Line

An exchange rate is the price of one nation's currency in terms of another nation's currency. Like other prices, exchange rates are determined by the forces of supply and demand. For example, if the demand for German deutsche marks increases, then the price of deutsche marks will increase relative to the U.S. dollar. If the supply of deutsche marks increases, then the price of deutsche marks will decline relative to the U.S. dollar.

When the exchange rate between two currencies changes, the relative prices of the imports and exports traded among countries using those currencies change. As a result, some groups benefit while others lose. In brief, a strong local currency means lower prices for imported goods; a weak local currency means that exported goods will become more affordable abroad.

Personal Economics

My first introduction to exchange rates came when I was a camp counselor in Canada one summer. I was paid 50 Canadian dollars that summer. When I went to my bank in the United States to deposit the paycheck, I was credited with only $45 in U.S. funds. Why? At that time, one Canadian dollar was worth only $0.90 in American funds. At that rate, $50 Canadian times 0.90 exchange rate equals $45 U.S.

Let's turn the situation around. What if I were a Canadian working in the United States and had been paid $50 in U.S. dollars? What would those U.S. funds have been worth in Canada? To convert U.S dollars into Canadian dollars, simply divide one by $0.90, the original exchange rate, to get $1.11. So, one U.S. dollar at that exchange rate equals $1.11 Canadian. $50 in U.S. funds times the $1.11 exchange rate would have been $55.55 in Canadian currency.

Check the newspaper for the current exchange rate for Canadian and U.S. dollars. Don't forget that you need two rates. If you've got only one exchange rate, simply divide one by that exchange rate to get the other rate.

Today's date: _____

$1 U.S.   = $_____ Canadian

$1 Canadian   = $_____ U.S.

As a college student, I studied in Spain for a semester. All the American students in my class watched the exchange rates closely. They were posted in the windows of most banks. We were interested in the value of the American dollar, since we wanted to exchange U.S. dollars for the Spanish pesetas needed to buy anything in Spain. When I arrived, the exchange rate was $1 U.S.=65 Spanish pesetas. By the end of the semester, it had edged up to $1 U.S.=70 Spanish pesetas. The U.S. dollar had gotten stronger, and the Spanish peseta weaker. This meant that our U.S. dollars were worth more at the end of the semester than they were at the beginning. We were happy. We could buy more in Spain!

(continued)

◆ INTERNATIONAL CURRENCY EXCHANGE: DOLLARS AND SENSE ◆ (continued)

Let's look at the math.

Exchange $100 U.S. for Spanish pesetas at $1 U.S.=65 Spanish pesetas.

$100 U.S.=_____ Spanish pesetas.

Exchange $100 U.S. for Spanish pesetas at $1 U.S.=70 Spanish pesetas.

$100 U.S.=_____ Spanish pesetas.

At the same time, Spanish students studying in the United States would have been unhappy that the Spanish peseta was getting weaker relative to the U.S. dollar. What was the exchange rate for Spanish pesetas in U.S. dollars at that time? If you forget how to calculate it, reread the Canadian example on the previous page.

Start of semester: 1 Spanish peseta=$____ U.S.

End of semester: 1 Spanish peseta=$____ U.S.

How much would Spanish students studying in the United States have received if they had converted 1,000 pesetas into U.S. dollars at the beginning of the semester? And another 1,000 pesetas into U.S. dollars at the end of the semester?

Start of semester
1,000 Spanish pesetas=$____ U.S.

End of semester
1,000 Spanish pesetas=$____ U.S.

Simple moral: If one currency gets stronger (appreciates), it can be exchanged for more of the other currency. If it gets weaker (depreciates), it can be exchanged for less of the other currency. As one currency appreciates, the other automatically depreciates, and vice versa!

Beyond the Bottom Line

Exchange rates affect imports and exports. Why?

Assume that today's newspaper quotes the following exchange rates:

1 Japanese yen = $0.00753 U.S.

$1 U.S.   = 132.75 yen

Consider what this means for sales of Japanese stereos and American computers. Assume that the price of a Japanese-made stereo is 100,000 yen in Japan. The price of an American-made computer is $1,000 in the United States. Assume also that Japanese producers export their stereos to the United States and that American producers export their computers to Japan. (And assume that there are no costs associated with this trade.)

Answer the following questions:

1. What is the current price of the Japanese-made stereo in the United States? $_____

2. What is the current price of the U.S.-made computer in Japan? _____ yen.

Now, if the U.S. dollar gets stronger relative to the Japanese yen, consider what will happen to the prices of these exports and imports. Assume that $1 U.S. is now worth 150 yen. The **domestic prices** of stereos (100,000 yen) and computers ($1,000) have not changed; only the **exchange rates**, and thus the **export/import prices** of these goods, have changed.

3. What is the new exchange rate for 1 Japanese yen? $_____ U.S.

4. What is the new price of the Japanese-made stereo in the United States? $_____

5. What is the new price of the American-made computer in Japan? _____ yen.

(continued)

◆ INTERNATIONAL CURRENCY EXCHANGE: DOLLARS AND SENSE ◆ (continued)

6. Compare the new prices to the original prices of Japanese stereos in the United States and U.S. computers in Japan. What has happened?

_____

_____

7. What do you think will happen to imports and exports in both countries as a result of these new export/import prices? In other words, what conclusion can you reach about the effect of changing exchange rates on exports and imports?

_____

_____

8. Complete these summary statements:

(a) If your currency gets stronger relative to another currency, exports will _____

and imports will _____ because _____.

(b) If your currency gets weaker relative to another currency, exports will _____

and imports will _____ because _____.

Special Bonus Question: Which of the following players would love to see a strong U.S. dollar relative to foreign currencies? Which would hate to see a strong U.S. dollar?

Player	Love/Hate	Explanation
Foreign producer of American imports		
American consumer		
American producer/exporter		
Foreign tourist in U.S.		
American tourist abroad		
Foreign consumer		

(continued)

◆ INTERNATIONAL CURRENCY EXCHANGE: DOLLARS AND SENSE ◆ *(continued)*

 Internet Economics

Up-to-the-minute currency exchange rates are easy to find on the Net. Lots of sites can tell you how many Italian lira or Russian rubles or Danish kroners you can get for $1 U.S. Several sites allow you to actually make a transaction!

At **www.xe.net/ucc**, all of the major currencies are listed with their current exchange rates and a conversion feature that enables you to see how much you can get for your money. So try it.

$1,000 U.S.=

_____ British pounds

_____ German marks

_____ Japanese yen

_____ Hong Kong dollars

_____ Greek drachmas

Denomination worth least relative to U.S. dollar:

_____

Because: _____

_____

A fascinating development in the history of currency exchange is the planned consolidation of several European currencies into one, the Euro. It's a move designed to increase trade, decrease costs, and promote economic growth, stability, and unity within the European Union (EU). (The EU is a free-trade organization, similar to NAFTA.) Not surprisingly, it's highly controversial. The United Kingdom, for example, will not shed the pound in favor of the Euro. Read all about the European Union and the Euro at **www.europa.eu.int**.

After checking out this site, answer the following questions:

When did the Euro make its first official appearance?

_____

When will ordinary citizens be eligible to obtain Euro notes and coins?

_____

What countries are members of the EU?

_____

_____

Which countries are not members of the EU?

_____

_____

Do you think the adoption of a single European currency is a good idea? Why or why not?

_____

_____

_____

Appendix I
A Very Different Kind of
Stock Market Project

To the Teacher

This is a long-term project designed to fulfill at least two objectives:

1. Students will see that investing in the stock market can be profitable, unprofitable, fun, exasperating, predictable, mystifying, and that the real world—in the form of commissions, capital gains taxes, market ups and downs, and so forth—can have a considerable impact on investment performance.

2. Students will experience for themselves that knowledge is power in the stock market—investors who don't have good reasons for their specific investments generally don't stay successful, or stay investing, or stay lucky, for very long.

   Before copying the simulation pages, add a due date in the box at the top of page 83. The date should be several months after the beginning of the simulation.

Name_____ Date_____

◆ A VERY DIFFERENT KIND OF STOCK MARKET PROJECT ◆

Starting Date: September _____

Due Date: _____ Your project should include records, comparisons, and analysis. In addition, updates, featuring written summaries, may be due periodically.

Objective: Become an investor. Buy and sell stocks as you see fit, based on *specific* information. Monitor, chart, and analyze your success (or lack thereof) throughout the semester.

Ground Rules for Investing

Congratulations! You have just inherited $_____ Use this amount to buy/sell stocks based on logical reasons and specific sources. Excess funds will be put in a money market cash account earning 0 percent annually.

1. You may buy/sell only stocks and bonds that are listed in the daily newspaper and are actively traded on the major exchanges: NYSE, American, NASDAQ. You should make at least one transaction per week.

2. You may buy or sell at the previous day's published closing price only.

3. Whenever you buy or sell a stock, you must pay a 1 percent **commission**.

4. If you sell at a profit (after deducting for all commissions), you must pay a **capital gains tax** on the profit (only) of 20 percent. You don't have to pay taxes on losses.

5. Record all transactions on the day you make them. Include commissions and capital gains, if applicable, and give **specific reasons** (with sources of information) why you made that transaction. An example follows:

On 9/16/96 I bought 2,000 shares of IBM common stock @ 105 because they came out with a new product line ("PC Beautiful"), which some industry experts believe should attract considerable attention in the PC market. Source: WSJ 9/15/96.

Note: The *Wall Street Journal* is a great source of information, but so are *Smart Money, Business Week, Fortune, Hoovers, CNN,* the Internet, your parents, your broker, even your friends. Just make sure they give you specific information, and **cite it!**

6. On at least a weekly basis, track and compare your portfolio record and selected stocks and bonds to other key indices, like the Dow Jones 30 Industrials, S&P 500, and so forth. Use computer-generated graphs, charts, and spreadsheets. *Tip:* Percent increases/decreases are usually the best indicators of performance.

7. Analyze your portfolio: What went wrong/ right? Why?

Final Words

- You will not be graded on the performance of your portfolio. You will be graded on the accuracy, completeness, and aggressiveness of your project and, especially, the quality of your analysis.

- You may consult with each other for ideas, but you must do your own work when it comes to making buy/sell decisions and producing the project.

- Cite all of your sources, and be specific!

- There will be no extensions.

- Good luck!

APPENDIX II

◆ FINALLY, UNDERSTANDING INTEREST AND INTEREST RATES ◆

A friend of mine pursued a career in banking. She told me that the single most useful thing she learned in introductory economics was the concept of interest. Well, you needn't be a banker or an economist to understand the importance of interest or interest rates. Anyone who has ever borrowed money or plans to borrow money—and that's most of us!—ought to understand interest, since that's money out of your pocket. Pay only part of your credit card bill? You owe interest. Get a car loan? Pay interest. Take out a mortgage? Pay lots of interest! Lend money to someone? Get interest.

What exactly is interest? **Interest** is the price you pay a lender for borrowing money. The price is typically quoted in percentages. It is usually calculated on an annual basis. The amount you must pay back to the lender includes your interest, as well as the money you borrowed, called the **principal**. *Example:* I borrow $10,000 from the bank at 10 percent interest, payable in one year. In one year's time, I will owe $10,000 principal plus $1,000 interest, or $11,000 total.

How are interest rates determined? Interest rates, like the prices of goods and services, are determined by the forces of supply and demand. This means you can use graphs to see interest-rate fluctuations. For example, if lots of individuals or businesses are looking for loans, the demand for loans will increase (*D* curve shifts right). Consequently, so will the equilibrium interest rate of loans. On the other hand, if banks have lots of money available for loans because many people are saving money in the bank, the supply of loans will increase (*S* curve shifts right), and interest rates will decline.

Exercise: Try graphing, on a separate sheet of paper, the supply and demand for loans. Put quantity on the *x* axis, and interest rates, instead of price, on the *y* axis. What happens if the demand for loans declines because people are worried that the economy will slump? What happens if the supply for loans declines because people are consuming more and therefore saving less? In the first scenario, interest rates will decline. In the second, interest rates will increase.

Is interest all profit to the lender? Surprisingly, the answer is no. Inflation, a general increase in the price of all goods and services, eats up the value of money/loans. *Example:* If inflation increases 5 percent this year, then I will need $105 next year to buy what $100 bought me this year. So, am I willing to lend $100 out at 5 percent interest? Not likely. At a 5 percent interest rate, I am making no real profit, since I will be paid $105 next year. Accounting for inflation, that is worth exactly $100 today. If I want to make a real profit, I must charge more than 5 percent. If I charge 15 percent interest, then my real profit—my real interest rate—is 10 percent. *Lesson:* The real interest rate is the stated market, or nominal, interest rate, minus the expected rate of inflation.

What's the significance of interest rates? Real interest rates represent real (after inflation) profit to lenders, as well as the real cost of borrowing to debtors. Higher interest rates provide incentives for people to save more, because banks will pay savers higher interest rates for deposits. They also encourage people to borrow less, because debt is more expensive. Lower interest rates provide incentives for people to save less and to borrow more.

(continued)

APPENDIX II

◆ FINALLY, UNDERSTANDING INTEREST AND INTEREST RATES ◆ *(continued)*

Why do lenders have to charge interest at all? There are two reasons: (1) inflation; (2) people must be compensated for deferring the use of resources from the present to the future. Remember our discussion of tradeoffs? **Opportunity cost** is the value of the foregone option. *Example:* If I decide to lend you $1,000, my opportunity cost is what I could have done with that $1,000, like going on a shopping spree. To compensate me for passing up that opportunity, you must pay me interest. If my foregone opportunity was using the $1,000 to buy a U.S. savings bond earning 6 percent interest, you must compensate me by agreeing to pay at least 6 percent interest when I lend the $1,000 to you instead. So, even if there's 0 percent inflation, lenders will always charge some interest to compensate for the fact that they are deferring the use of resources—their money—so that they can lend it to you now.

Are all borrowers the same? Do banks charge the same interest to all borrowers? No! If you have significant assets (own a lot of things), an excellent record of paying your bills on time,

and a big salary, you will pay a lower interest rate than someone who doesn't have much in the way of assets and income and is often late paying bills. Why? Lenders determine interest rates in part on the chances of repayment. The only way that lenders will lend money to someone who poses a risk of defaulting on the repayment is if the lender will earn a higher interest rate. This is known as the relationship between risk and reward. The higher the risk of default by the borrower, the greater must be the reward to the lender to make the risk worth taking. Despite the fact that people with lower incomes usually pay more interest than borrowers with higher incomes, the risk-reward relationship actually makes sense. Lenders must be compensated for taking a greater risk; otherwise, they won't lend the money!

Bottom line: Interest rates are determined by the supply and demand for loans. These in turn are influenced by inflation, opportunity costs, and risk/reward.

APPENDIX III

◆ CALCULATING INFLATION:
YOUR OWN PERSONAL CONSUMER PRICE INDEX (CPI) ◆

Background

The federal government measures inflation by checking each month the prices of a so-called market basket of goods and services that an average urban household might buy. The results are factored into the Consumer Price Index, or CPI. This can be used to compare the price level in one year with price levels in earlier or later periods. So when the government reports that inflation rose 5 percent last year, that means that the overall cost of this market basket increased by 5 percent.

Here's the chance for you and a partner to produce your own CPI. For the two of you, it's going to be more accurate and useful than the official CPI! Ideally, this project can extend over the entire school year, although it can also be undertaken over the course of one semester.

Directions

Make a list of the goods and services you and/or your partner typically buy and use in a given month—your market basket. Record them on the chart on the next page. Consider different foods, articles of clothing, household products, toiletries, gas for your car, bus or subway tokens, trips to the movie theater, restaurants—anything you purchase on a regular or semiregular basis.

Once you've made your list, go out with your partner and buy (or get prices for) all of the goods on your list. If there are some services you typically pay for, like visiting a video arcade or

going to a concert, make those visits and pay for them as well.

Keep close track of the actual prices you paid for these goods and services and the dates you purchased them. If at all possible, try to buy everything on the same date, like the first of the month. *Note:* This may take some planning and some specialization of labor with your partner. But even if you can't buy everything on the same day, find out what the items in your market basket would have cost on the same day. You can do that by visiting some stores or making some phone calls to check prices. In addition, if you go to a concert only twice a year, find out the total annual cost (for example, $20 per ticket for the first concert plus $10 per ticket for the second show) and divide by 12 to get a prorated monthly cost.

Now, add up what it cost you to buy all the items in your market basket on a given day in the first month—say, October. Then, exactly a month later (November), repeat the exercise. Buy exactly the same goods and services at the same stores, if possible, or simply check to see what the same goods and services cost. Then, record the prices and calculate your total expenditure.

Do the same exercise once a month for the duration of the semester or the year. You can also do your buying, or price checking, on a weekly basis if you don't have a lot of time left in your course. Complete the chart on the next page and answer the questions that follow.

(continued)

APPENDIX III

◆ CALCULATING INFLATION:
YOUR OWN PERSONAL CONSUMER PRICE INDEX (CPI) ◆ *(continued)*

Our Market Basket of Goods and Services	

Time	Total cost ($) of market basket of goods and services
Month 1 (Date:_____)	
Month 2 (Date:_____)	
Month 3 (Date:_____)	
Month 4 (Date:_____)	
Month 5 (Date:_____)	
Month 6 (Date:_____)	

Questions and Analysis

1. What was the dollar change in total cost from one month to the next? More importantly, what was the percent change from one month to the next?

2. What was the percent change from the first month's to the last month's total cost of your market basket?

3. Now, annualize the percent change. To do this properly, you must remember there are 52 weeks in a year, and if you only have 13 weeks of data, you must multiply percent changes by 4 to yield *annualized* percentages. If your project covered six months and the cost of the total market basket rose 2 percent, then the annual 12-month change would be twice 2 percent, or a 4 percent rise in your consumer price index.

4. What was the range of prices of individual goods and services? Which individual goods and services rose the most? Which rose the least? Did any items drop in price? Calculate percent, not dollar, changes to come up with the most meaningful answers.

5. Compare your results, specifically the annualized percent change of your market basket, with the official CPI, which can be found periodically in any major newspaper or on the Internet. Did your consumer price index differ from the official CPI? By how much? Why? In what ways do you think that your CPI had fewer or more specific items found or not found in the average urban family's market basket?

       Activities for Economics Education

Name_____ Date_____

APPENDIX IV

◆ Calculating Unemployment:
Your Own Local Unemployment Rate ◆

Background

The federal government measures unemployment by sampling approximately 60,000 representative households each month. The government wants to determine the employment status of anyone over the age of 16 who is not in prison, in a mental hospital, or on active duty in the military.

These representatives of the entire U.S. population are then classified into one of three categories: (1) Employed—working; (2) Unemployed—jobless, looking for a job, and available for work; (3) All others—not in the labor force. The unemployment rate (percent) is calculated by dividing the unemployed (2) by the total labor force [(1)+(2)].

Here's the chance for you and a partner to produce your own local unemployment rate. For the two of you and for the class, it could be more meaningful than the official U.S. unemployment rate.

Directions:

Open the local phone book and arbitrarily choose a page. Now, divide up the names. You and your partner should each make at least 25 phone calls to different households that you don't know personally. Identify yourself clearly to each person who answers:

Hi, I am _____, a student at _____ High School. My economics class is undertaking a very short phone survey to estimate the local unemployment rate. Would you be willing to answer about five questions?

If they aren't willing, politely reassure them that this is a legitimate, class-sponsored survey, and give them the names of your teacher and principal. If they still won't participate in the survey, thank them for their time, and try again with someone else. Always be courteous and respectful, even if the person on the other end of line is not.

Ask the following questions about all household members, keeping a careful record of each phone call:

1. Age: _____

2. Gender: _____

3. Marital status: _____

4. Highest level of education: _____

5. Do you have a paying job? _____

  A) If yes, what kind? _____
    End of survey

  B) If no, what was your last paying job?

  _____

  Are you able to work? _____

  Are you looking for work?_____

    If yes, End of survey

    If no, reasons for not looking

    _____

End of survey

(continued)

Name_____ Date_____

APPENDIX IV

◆ CALCULATING UNEMPLOYMENT:
YOUR OWN LOCAL UNEMPLOYMENT RATE ◆ *(continued)*

Questions and Analysis

1. How many people did you and your partner survey? _____

   What was the age span? _____

   What was the gender breakout? _____

   Marital status? _____

   Education range? _____

2. How many people had a paying job? _____

   How many people did not have a paying job? _____

3. Of the people without work, how many were unable to work? _____

   How many were not looking for work? _____

4. Of the people not looking for work, what were their reasons for not looking? _____

   _____

   _____

   _____

5. Calculate your local unemployment rate by dividing the number of the officially unemployed (jobless, but able and looking) by the labor force (the unemployed plus the employed).

   _____

6. How does your local unemployment rate compare with the official U.S. unemployment rate? (This can be found periodically in any major newspaper or on the Internet.) Is the job picture in your region better or worse than in the United States as a whole? Why? How representative do you think your sample was of the population in your town? In the United States as a whole?

   _____

   _____

   _____

   _____

   _____

   _____

7. What conclusions can you draw, if any, about the link between unemployment and age? Or unemployment and gender? Or unemployment and marital status? Or unemployment and education?

   _____

   _____

   _____

   _____

   _____

Share Your Bright Ideas with Us!

We want to hear from you! Your valuable comments and suggestions will help us meet your current and future classroom needs.

Your name_____Date_____

School name_____Phone_____

School address_____

Grade level taught_____Subject area(s) taught_____Average class size_____

Where did you purchase this publication?_____

Was your salesperson knowledgeable about this product?   Yes_____   No_____

What monies were used to purchase this product?

____School supplemental budget   ____Federal/state funding   ____Personal

Please "grade" this Walch publication according to the following criteria:

Quality of service you received when purchasing	A	B	C	D	F
Ease of use	A	B	C	D	F
Quality of content	A	B	C	D	F
Page layout	A	B	C	D	F
Organization of material	A	B	C	D	F
Suitability for grade level	A	B	C	D	F
Instructional value	A	B	C	D	F

COMMENTS:_____

_____

What specific supplemental materials would help you meet your current—or future—instructional needs?

_____

Have you used other Walch publications? If so, which ones?_____

May we use your comments in upcoming communications?   ____Yes   ____No

Please **FAX** this completed form to **207-772-3105**, or mail it to:

Product Development, J. Weston Walch, Publisher, P.O. Box 658, Portland, ME 04104-0658

We will send you a **FREE GIFT** as our way of thanking you for your feedback. **THANK YOU!**